How to be Selfish
(And other uncomfortable advice)

By Olga Levancuka

06/16

PRAIRIE DU CHIEN MEMORIAL LIBRARY

125 S. Wacouta Ave.

Prairie du Chien, WI 53821

608-326-6211

Mon-Thu 9-8 Fri 9-5 Sat 9-1

Copyright © 2012 by Olga Levancuka

All rights reserved. No part of this book may be reproduced, stored or transmitted by any means – whether auditory, graphical, mechanical or electronic – without written permission of both publisher and author, except in the case of brief excerpts used in critical articles and reviews. Unauthorized reproduction of any part of this work is illegal and is punishable by law.

Cover Design © Reyl Design Group 2012

How to be Selfish (And other uncomfortable advice), Olga Levancuka.

For bulk purchases for sales promotions, premiums, fund-raising, or educational use please inquire via www.OlgaLevancuka.com

ISBN-13: 978-1468115987

ISBN-10: 1468115987

CONTENTS

Prairie du Chien
Memorial Library
125 Wacouta Ave.
Prairie du Chien WI 53821

PART ONE: WHY DO YOU NEED THIS BOOK?

An introduction

Have you ever owned a hamster? If so, you probably watched it running on a wheel, round and round, going nowhere and not realizing it.

Can you relate to that? That feeling of being trapped? That feeling that maybe there's a bigger world out there? How do you step out into it?

People run on wheels too, non-stop. Unlike hamsters, we don't have owners who buy our wheels for us, but we do all get gently squeezed into wheels that we didn't ask for and that perhaps we don't even notice.

The first wheel, at school, sets us running and running and running... Until one day we are ready to go to university or start working. Then we get a job... and we are running and running and running and running again. We're told we have choices, yet the pressure to do what we're supposed to, to do what a 'good little boy or girl' would do, is so strong. Do we have any choice at all?

The wheel you climb into is often influenced by something outside of you - whatever your parents told you, or whatever you have learned is the socially acceptable path to take.

And there it is - a job, a family, kids at school… running and running and running and always wondering, 'is this all there is?'

That's how my mother lived, until one day she was given five days to live and almost died in surgery. That's how suddenly we can get thrown off the wheel.

Are you perhaps ready to try something more dangerous, something less comfortable and less predictable? Are you ready to find out what you really want, and how to get it?

Even though everyone – your parents, your teachers, your God perhaps - tells you not to be selfish, you still want so much. So what now? Perhaps it's time to try the unthinkable. Perhaps it's time to experiment with selfishness.

What is selfishness?

Does selfishness have negative associations for you? Does it conjure up an image of someone mean, like a fairytale ogre perhaps?

I'm here to tell you that there is another way to be selfish. Selfishness is about helping yourself, yes. It's about satisfying the deep desires within you that cause so much heartache.

However, being selfish can also be the best way to improve the lives of people around you. Being strong and joyful and sure of yourself is a gift to the rest of the world, as well as to yourself.

I've never lived for others. You might say I'm selfish. Do you know what I've discovered? By living my own life with joy, I've enriched the lives of so many around me! By contaminating them with my happiness and success, people around me have been inspired to follow their own dreams.

If I spent my life feeling guilty and beating myself up for wanting too much or taking up too much space, would that really help the people I love? If I try to live through other people, isn't that a burden that I'm placing on them?

You do not need to take on someone else's problems to help them. That way, you deny them their own experience, even if that experience means pain. By appreciating them for who they are and treating them as an equal human being, while living your own, full life ... boy, you'll touch their hearts and inspire them to move mountains.

What will this book do for you?

If you want a one word answer - nothing! Because the changes that you make to your life after reading this will be entirely up to you.

You won't be alone. I am here to help you. Imagine, as you read, that we are just having a conversation over a cup of tea. I'll be sharing some very personal stories and telling you about my (often strange) life experiences and what I've learned from them.

You will bring your own life experience to everything that you read here. All our lives on this planet are so different, perhaps you and I will have hardly any experiences in common. What we do have in common, is that we are facing the same challenge: the world is full of people telling us what to do. I am planning to help you tell them where to stick it, and how to find your own unique way through all the obstacles that life throws at you.

What will we talk about?

In this book, I'm going to bring up all the topics that you're not supposed to bring up at dinner parties. The awkward, difficult, controversial, personal ones. That is…

Religion

Karma

Body image

Money

Emotions

Childhood pain

……and a little bit of Energy.

I am going to show you a new side to these themes, and force you – gently ;) - to sort through what you think about them. I mean, what YOU, your precious self, really thinks, not what you've been told to think all your life by your parents, by society, by the media, or by whoever has been drip-drip-dripping ideas into your mind without you noticing.

Tell me I'm wrong, pleeeeease!

During our imaginary conversation, perhaps you will disagree with me on some topics. Perhaps you'll disagree with everything I say?

Good. I really want you to. The aim of this book is for you to rebel against things other people tell you; against the ideas that you are handed on a plate.

In my work as a Life Coach, I've been reminded how reluctant people are to say that they disagree with someone in a position of 'authority'. Let me give you an example.

I once ran an exercise during a workshop. This workshop was taking place in a Shoreditch fashion boutique, so we were surrounded by beautiful corsets and dresses. I picked up a charming red dress and I turned to my audience and stated, 'this dress is black'.

The purpose of the exercise was to provoke a debate, so I could explain a point I wanted to make about trusting your intuition. I was honestly expecting them to say something along the lines of 'Olga, contrary to what you say, the dress is actually bright red'.

Instead, they said nothing. They didn't contradict me, they didn't argue.

I was in shock. I realized that this group had been attending my workshops for some time now and they had come to believe every single word I said, however ridiculous or obviously untrue.

Perhaps I should have been flattered. These are clients who have told me that they've achieved amazing, tangible results using advice I've given to them. That's why they trusted me so much.

Despite this, their reaction – or lack of reaction – to the exercise made me tear out my hair. It was everything I try to fight against, and encourage my clients to fight against. They were following me blindly!

That's when I knew I had to work harder to shake people up and make them really question whether they're doing something because they believe it is right for them, or because someone else has told them it is.

People want to believe. If one bit of 'preaching' works for them, they believe that the next thing their 'preacher' tells them must be true.

But in the end, disagreeing with me and coming up with their own answers is what makes my clients the successful, vibrant, fulfilled people that they are. So as you read, please kick and scream and throw the book across the room. Be bad. Don't just do what I say. All I want is for you to listen and make your own choices.

PART TWO: MY WEIRD AMAZING LIFE

Hello, I'm Olga

Since we're going to spend some time together as you read this book, perhaps you'd like to know who I am. I'm going to be your guide, a bit like the friend who's always there for you but who sometimes annoys you by pushing you out of your comfort zone. So, who is this Olga, whispering to you, challenging you?

I'll tell you stories about myself along the way, but here are a few little nuggets to break the ice. It's sad that a book is one-way, because I'd love to hear your story too! Perhaps we'll meet one day and I will. So for now, here I am...

Ideas can kill

I was born in what was known as the Soviet Union, or USSR, and is now known as Russia. When I was very young it was a time of transformation – the last days of Communism. But my parents were still Communists –

one believed in the cause, the other pretended to as a matter of survival as at that time, expressing the wrong opinion could get you killed.

So I was in a constant state of fear about doing or saying the 'wrong' thing. My clients sometimes complain that I don't talk about myself or my beliefs enough. I guess that's a minor echo left behind from that time.

That's how powerful ideas can be. Ideas can kill. Ideas can silence you. Yet they can also help you change your life and the world beyond recognition.

A day that shaped me

Let me tell you about one particular day when I was six years old. I was living in a large apartment at the time, just me and my parents. This was unusual – my father was a military man and in favour with the 'higher-ups' who made the decisions about who lived where, so we lived in relative luxury. We had a whole apartment to ourselves in the centre of town.

But many people I knew lived in the communal flats that were popular in the USSR at the time. In those tall grey blocks, four families would live in one single apartment. I know that sounds horrific to some, but if you have never known anything else, it isn't so bad.

In fact, I'd often visit friends living in these flats, and I loved it. I loved the fact I wasn't alone but at the same time I could totally disappear and go unnoticed, almost as if I didn't exist.

But one day, I was shocked out of that dreamy, child-like existence.

It was a very cloudy winter day and I was returning home from school. I loved my walks, they made me feel free. I didn't have to communicate with anyone or experience any of the stresses that I had at home or school.

On that particular walk, I saw something. I don't remember it entirely, but I know this much: I saw a few boys I knew – who lived in one of those communal flats. They were trying to kill another boy.

They wanted to know what it was like to kill another human being, so they picked a victim in my class. That day I was the witness of an attempted murder.

The children did not know how to go about it, so they decided to pierce our classmate's brain with a pen through his nose.

I don't remember what was going through my mind but I followed them and watched it happen for a while.

I am pretty sure I asked them to stop but I didn't dare to interfere physically. Eventually, I left and went home.

It was as if I was not actually present at the scene. Instead, I was an observer with no opinion whatsoever. It was like watching a movie in very, very slow motion.

If you've ever been in a car accident you may have experienced a similar effect, when time seems to slow down and you do nothing. You simply watch, like you are incapable of doing anything at all.

Whatever happened next, I know that I was the one blamed for giving away the names of the guilty parties. I don't remember much, I do remember that I didn't care that they blamed me. I never cared about following the pack mentality - even when I was so young and helpless.

The boy survived, luckily. He went on to have a life – some of it bad, some of it good. He went to prison for robbery some years later and then went on to be an evangelical Christian, which his parents were delighted about.

That day, when I came so close to seeing death, stayed with me for some time and raised lots of questions in my little head. Before that day I did not believe that death existed, or that such a thing could be even possible.

So, something changed. I don't believe it changed for the worse, but it definitely changed.

Learning to be bad and enjoying being mad

On another walk later that winter, I was strolling along a path where snow was slowly melting and turning from that beautiful white crisp state into a horrible brown semi-wet consistency. The weather had slightly warmed up so there was no fresh snow to cover the natural ugliness of the melting sludge.

I was walking behind people, and I was trying to walk in a way that would splash sludge over the backs of their legs, making their clothes dirty. I was wondering whether they'd notice me.

I gave myself a brownie point every time I achieved my mission and got away with it.

I knew it was wrong. I found myself enjoying being a 'bad' person after always playing the role of the good girl. It is strange to think that I thought such behaviour was bad, considering the really bad thing I'd seen the other children do! I'd had a rather strict upbringing, so even a little bit of badness like that felt very wicked. I realised it also felt good.

So, as I was indulging in this thuggish behaviour, I had sort of a revelation.

I suddenly had this sense that I was a little star which had fallen to earth. I knew for sure in that second that anyone in my presence would feel love, warmth and I could share with them that 'happiness' I so often feel for no apparent reason.

Did I mention I was a weird kid?

I was so excited, I rushed home and waited for my parents to come back from work, then insisted they should change my name to 'zvezdochka' or 'zvaigznite' – both words mean 'little star' in Russian and Latvian respectively.

They thought I was mad. I still think I was onto something good, even though it was a childish fantasy. If you feel happy for no reason, or if your mind wanders off along strange trains of thought... why not follow and see where it leads?

Fitting in (a little, anyway)

Still, you can't live in a fantasy all the time, or you'd be very lonely. There is a world out there and you have to find a way of living in it. I learned how to do this in a very awkward way.

Some of my clients will recognize a story here that I share far too often. When I was about seven years old, I wanted to reach out to others, so I made a decision to become more communicative.

These days I am a very direct person, but at that young age I was the shyest kid there is. It was unbearable at times, and I wanted to learn to beat my shyness once and for all. I got hold of a book of exercises to help people become more communicative and social. I followed the exercises eagerly. I would go up to strangers in the street in the middle of a bitter winter and ask them 'Do you know where the crocodiles live?' or 'Have you ever seen a crocodile? Where can I see one?'

My social skills have improved over the years, you'll be happy to hear, yet I was and still am one of the shyest people you'll meet. I've learned to deal with it, but my friends find it part of my charm that I blush ever so easily.

So I forced myself to become more social and to reach out to people. And, bit by bit, I made friends. Eventually, I went abroad to study. When Communism fell and my home country was all in a bit of a mess, my parents advised me to stay there, as it would be dangerous to return home.

So I built a life away from home, and eventually fell in love. Everything was good.

Love and death

In my twenties, I thought my life was perfect. I was running a very successful lingerie business and I was married to the man of my dreams. Then came the most terrible news I have ever heard: my husband was diagnosed with cancer.

Things happened fast, and he died soon after. So there I was, alone and in a state of utter shock and grief.

I had to start again, when I thought I'd built the life I was going to live forever.

With the support of my gorgeous friends, I put myself back together again. I had to put myself back together – there was no other option.

Maybe it sounds impossible to come back from something like that and be happy again. I did. You too can move on from anything, even the worst tragedy, and live a beautiful life.

Tea and other little things

Writing this book has been a wonderful experience. I will admit though, I have spent a lot of time struggling to write it. Or rather, I've been enjoying my life sooooo much I hardly had time to write.

Obviously, I managed to make time (or you wouldn't be reading this). As I write, I'm realising that I am - probably for the first time since losing my husband - consciously happy. I am happy to be alive.

I am happy to be sitting and being, just slowly drinking my cup of tea and listening to my own breath. Or annoying the hell out of my partner by continuously pinching him (don't worry, not too hard) and watching his reaction. Or just watching a movie, or opening at a book and, instead of reading it, just looking at the shape of the letters.

Material things

My friends and clients all know I'm a shopaholic. I don't think there's anything wrong with loving beautiful things, and making money so I can buy them. In the middle of a global financial crisis, saying that will not be popular. Screw popular! This is who I am. What do you think?

Up and down (and up again)

I'm a Life Coach these days, but my passions have taken me in many different directions in the course of my career. After all, how could I teach about life if I haven't lived it, in all its messy glory?

I've worked as a translator for a major oil company.

I've worked for the Mafia (I won't go into details, for obvious reasons – I don't know about you but I don't really want a horse's head in my bed, or to end up getting arrested.)

I've made a fortune as an entrepreneur, then lost everything when my husband died, as my business collapsed when my life fell apart with grief.

I've gone from a little girl with no friends, to a businesswoman with a multi-million dollar lingerie business. I've been a cancer patient and I've wept at the deathbed of my husband. I've lost a child. I've been a sex addict. I've worked in an AIDS laboratory and a cancer research lab (I've got a medical background).

So, let's say, I've lived a lot of life in my thirty-odd years on this planet. I've lost more than I ever thought possible, and then gained even more than that.

Over to you

This book comes into your hands from someone who's been so poor it sounds almost funny, like a sentimental passage from Dickens about a little orphan child – I honestly had to eat rotten garlic sometimes during my childhood.

I've also been very wealthy, and I do find making money a really exciting thing to do. I know both sides of this coin very well.

So, here I am, like you in some ways and very different in others – another human being with my own failures and victories writing a book about life for you, a person with your own struggles and fears.

Please take from it what you need the most, and read it whenever you have doubts about your life. If I can come back from a dark place, so can you. You can live a truly beautiful life.

In my darkest moments, I wish I could've had someone to help me see that there is light at the end of the tunnel. I wish I'd had something to ease the pain of loss and grief, and to help me understand the control I can have over seemingly uncontrollable events.

This is what I'm hoping to give you here. I want you to take that love of life that I have now and keep it with you at all times. Life is great, I promise you.

I always knew it deep down, even though there were times when I wanted to take my own life.

Now I've learned to embrace this beautiful world. How about we try and do that together, right now?

It's over to you now.

PART THREE: The big scary topics

Now you know about me, let's get right down to the hard stuff: your beliefs. Are you ready?

Religion

Are you religious? If not, you could skip this part. But if you wonder whether perhaps you should be religious, that you might be missing out – then read on. If you picked up this book in the first place and read this far, maybe you're looking for something that you're not getting from religion.

So, why religion? Why do people follow one faith system or another?

I once heard an amazing explanation: 'I only became a Catholic because the naughty sense of guilt I feel simply by doing something I enjoy only gives me extra pleasure.'

I'm guessing that there is probably more to it than that for many people!

When it comes to this life, the choices we face are limitless. And so are the responsibilities and the stress involved in these choices. This is where religion sometimes comes in. Religion offers a system of rules that tell us which choices are good ones. It lays down laws that break the world's infinite possibilities down into something more manageable.

Imagine that one day, you wake up on a beautiful island. The sun is shining, the birds are singing. The weather is lovely and warm, and you can feel a soft breeze brushing your skin ever so gently.

You think 'Oh MY! At last I've found my own oasis!'

You are so overwhelmed with happiness that you're almost breathless for a moment. Then very shortly after this rush of euphoria, something starts to distract you. You notice that there is a small insect-like creature playing with your big toe. You don't know what it is.

For a moment you think 'How sweet'.

Then you start to worry that the insect is about to bite you, because you've just noticed it has a strange formation on its head that looks like a very big pair of piercing teeth.

You are not sure what to do. Panic sets in. You suddenly notice you are completely naked. You start worrying. You notice there is nothing around to protect yourself with, you are in the middle of a beach and haven't taken any time to explore the island as it never crossed your mind that you might be in danger. Help!

You now notice there are other unknown creatures around you and you start worrying that the island might not be paradise after all, but a hostile, unknown place. You now start feeling really, really afraid. You do not know what to do.

The creatures look at you as if they are trying to figure out whether you are prey, a threat or one of them. You definitely 'know' you are about to be eaten, something just tells you so. Your fear takes over. What do you do?

What if all of this is just a product of your wild imagination? What if the creatures are simply afraid of you and are waiting to figure you out?

Sounds familiar? A little bit like elements of your life? Wouldn't it be so much easier if the scenario went something like this...

Imagine waking up on the same beautiful island. The sun is shining, the birds are singing. The weather is lovely and warm, and you can feel a soft breeze brushing your skin ever so gently. You think 'Oh MY! At last I've found my own oasis!' You are so overwhelmed with happiness that you're almost breathless for a moment. But very shortly after this rush of euphoria, something starts to distract you.

You notice there is a God-like figure (maybe even your mother or father) who looks really friendly, is aware of the fact you are naked and is holding out a beautiful robe for you to put on.

You notice that another person has brought you some food and drink. These lovely people explain everything you need to know about the island and how you can enjoy it, in exchange for the agreement that you follow a few simple rules.

I mean the usual stuff - honour your father and your mother, do not murder, do not steal, do not bear false witness or covet your neighbour's wife/ox/clothes. I am sure the religion you're following - if you are not an atheist - will have some system of rules that you are supposed to follow.

You might be fine with that. You might feel a little lost without guidance. You need it. You need it to ensure your survival. You need to KNOW that what you're doing and believing is correct - if you feel unsure about anything, there is a God or Buddha or other spiritual leader you follow or respect who will know the answer. So you follow blindly and without questioning. But, hey - they are promising you eternal safety and comfort, and at this moment, when you are totally naked, this doesn't seem like much of a sacrifice.

You are saved from anxieties, confusion, fear and panic, so it is absolutely worth following the rules chosen by you religion.

Religion can offer an unlimited source of help and hope, which as humans, we constantly crave. It promises that there is someone out there who accepts you just the way YOU are and who loves us all unconditionally. Isn't that wonderful? I honestly believe that is amazing.

I'll tell you why. It's a pretty dark story, so bear with me.

As a teenager, I made a couple of unsuccessful suicide attempts. I was too afraid of the pain to really go for it, and mostly stuck with self-harm as a way of dealing with my life.

There was one time when I found the strength to go 'all the way'. I chose a day and I started working on a plan to murder myself. It was all going well – if that's the right way to describe it. I was around 12 or 13 years old.

My birthday party was on the 12th of May and I was planning on doing it straight after my birthday party, in order to avoid attracting any attention – as if that's possible with suicide.

I remember my birthday quite vividly.

The children were all gathered in my living room. That day, I received so many presents and I remember taking my time opening them before sitting down at the table. There was plenty of food. Everyone was happy and giggling.

One of my presents was some perfume, which I accidentally spilled all over my piano. I was so scared my parents would go mad at me. It's strange that I was worried about a telling-off, considering what I was planning to do. That's how irrational our fears can be.

Then this guy I fancied - so much - gave me a book with a fish symbol on the cover. He said it was a history book of some kind. I suspect his mother has chosen it on his behalf, but I was still upset to receive a weird book as a present. Luckily I did not know at the time that it was about religion.

Why would I have been cross if I'd known it was about Christianity? I was the most extreme atheist out there at that time. I'd even given some speeches on the subject at my school. Even at that age I had very strong views!

Once the party was over, I put off what I'd planned to do for a while and started to browse through the book. The story captivated me.

I did get very confused by the fact that Christians do not murder themselves like I was planning to do, but instead they tolerate, almost embrace suffering... that didn't seem to make sense.

Then I read that to kill oneself is like murdering an innocent, unprotected, vulnerable creature - because there is no one who can protect you from yourself.

Those words had a strong enough influence on me to make me rethink my plans – and I'm still here today!

Sometimes, when it feels like you have no one to turn to, religion may be your only salvation. You might say that Christianity saved me. So, in this next section, I'm not asking you to give up on your beliefs, if you have any. I merely ask you to see if you can suspend them temporarily and consider another way of thinking – let's call it a thought experiment.

I'm going to ask the question again: Why religion? And if you are religious, why have you chosen one religion over another?

Well, religion gives you a framework for your life and offers guidance. Because whatever it is you do, you want to be sure it is the right thing and that you are a good person. The religion you chose maybe appealed to you emotionally at the time. Or maybe you were brought up with it? Or perhaps it was just the 'nearest' religion to you – the religion of your community, or of people you've met in your life.

You might believe that by following certain religious traditions and rules you are better than others - or at least you feel accepted, included and 'part of the gang'. We all want to be respected, we want to be accepted and more than anything, we want to belong.

Religion also offers a sense of the spiritual - confirming the belief that we are not simply a highly-developed animal; we are more than that, because God says so.

We have a mind, we have a soul – don't we? Ah, but we want to be sure of this. We can't believe it just by listening to our own instincts and knowledge of ourselves. That doesn't seem valid – who are we to decide we are anything special?

No, we'll only accept 'proper' proof that we are a very special person. Proof from God, from a church, from a preacher or from someone in authority.

Question: What if you trusted your own heart instead? Don't you know that you're special, just on your own merits?

I know it can be hard to believe that we are 'enough'. When we grow up, we search for ways to make money and gain recognition. Or we spend hours preparing a meal for every single guest we've invited to a party, or dedicate our lives to looking after ill relatives or tidying up after other people, because it seems terrible and sinful to simply focus on our own needs.

Such troubles, no matter how necessary they are to us, may bring us down emotionally and, though we might not say so out loud, they make us feel less of a human being. We feel as though our life isn't fulfilled because all our time is spent thinking about other people.

We feel empty and pointless, like that hamster running and running on the same old wheel.

In the face of that emptiness, we want to feel reassured that we are special. We want some sort of confirmation that we are not simply animals. So we need to believe in something more.

We want to believe in something bigger and more important than we are. Possibly a creator of some sort, someone who could 'prove' that we are more than just physical beings. We crave the existence of something bigger than ourselves, someone who knows all the answers and can offer us respite from our busy, questioning minds.

If we don't feel like we are in control, we hope that someone else is.

While religion is partly about setting rules which offer a feeling of security, it is also about getting answers to some of the big, scary questions.

Religion is like a parent, who, even though he or she does not know all the answers, will give their child any answer just to keep them quiet. Or the passer-by who offers a tourist any old directions, just to get them and their huge rucksack out of the way.

Wrong or right is irrelevant. When you want an answer – you want one, and NOW!

During my childhood I'd constantly ask my parents about religion.

'Who is Christ? What other religions are out there?'

I was about five at the time and living a country ruled by a Communist government that didn't take kindly to religion. It was hard to find out about this stuff, although my parents explained it to me as best they could (and as quietly).

Most of my clients are aware that I am not a religious person. But I'm still a believer of sorts: I believe that our life is very real and that this is enough.

Most importantly I am aware of the fact that people want to believe.

'The kingdom of God is here within you' - ever heard that? Maybe you read it in a bible, or there is a similar saying in your religion?

That feeling of the divine inside you... have you considered that might just be you? No father or mother figure hovering above and beyond you but just your precious self? Like in John Lennon's Imagine: 'No hell below us...above us only sky.'

Could you be following rules that were created thousands of years ago and giving up who you are just to follow these rules – and all for someone who doesn't exist? Just consider that.

If your belief is that you are suffering because you are a sinner, and humans are all sinners, then you will continue suffering. I am aware that many religions put forward the idea that you are on earth because you are a sinner and you pay for your sins by tolerating pain or suffering. I once worked with a client, who rung me rather unexpectedly during our early sessions and shouted, 'Why me? What did I do to God? Why was my car stolen? What did I do wrong?'

If you follow a religion (whichever one it may be) and it enhances your experience of life, by all means continue with it. Life is a beautiful creation. We are creating the world around us all the time, every minute of every day, so you can make God real if that's what you want.

Do ask yourself carefully (in case you are really in denial): 'Why exactly have I chosen to follow this religion? What exactly was missing in my life that I found by following this particular religion?'

It may be that you felt lonely and unappreciated. It may be you were brought up like this and never ever questioned your beliefs.

For those who believe in Christianity, it is in the Bible (one of the multiple translations) that: 'the kingdom of God is here within you'.

Great words. You are the creator, you are God in your own right.

Look around, understand that you are also the creator of the world around you. You've made your life what it is today. I'll come back to this later.

The other theme I need to mention here is karma. Do you believe in karma? Then it's real. It's real to you. Your mind is so powerful that what you create in your head shapes the world around you. If you believe things that happen in your life are an echo of a past life, then that's what's real for you.

Do you really believe, or do you just want to believe because it's easier?

Karma is a brilliant excuse for laziness. It means you don't have to take responsibility to move your life forward. It makes sense of events that can seem chaotic, but it could be leading you to misunderstand your life.

More on that later. For now, just think about Buddhism - where everyone has a 'karma' and it is accepted that followers of this faith have to work hard and make sacrifices throughout their lives. Why exactly?

Why is it that your worth is decided as soon as you're born – whether as the lowest of the low, or as a saint? At the beginning of your life you haven't worked hard, or done anything wrong – your status shouldn't be predestined.

All - I repeat - ALL of your actions throughout your life will create something, good or bad. Not all of your creations will produce the results you expect, though.

Not all good deeds will produce beneficial results and not all evil actions will produce bad results. For example, let's compare the policemen and the terrorist. Are they really that different? The policemen may kill a terrorist in order to save lives of many, but he has still killed someone. Each believes that what they are doing is good.

That is a very hypothetical explanation. It's only here to give you a glimpse into the twisted world of good and evil that can arise when you think in terms of karma.

In the end, life is about you being a creative individual, fully responsible for your actions and thoughts.

You see, humans love rules, as they form a self-preservation mechanism. This was absolutely necessary at the beginning of human life, but we cannot forget that as humans, we constantly evolve.

Increasingly, religions are becoming nothing more than brilliant control mechanisms and – this is what I believe, do challenge me – could actually hinder your future development. Religion can stop you from having enriching experiences, whether it's something as simple as eating prawns or bacon, or seeing an amazing view at a time when you 'should' be working or praying.

As you already do with many things in your life (I suspect you eat fish and leave the bones, or you eat an egg without its shell) – take the best of what religion can offer you and 'eat' only what you need. However valuable religion can be to you, it is your own eternal light and your personal inner truth that counts the most. It is your soul which warms those around you, it is your hands that are cooking dinner for your children. The examples are endless. You are the strength - start accepting it. That way, you will no longer need to makes choices based on fear, for you will know that the strength and knowledge is yours and comes from your own soul.

You'll do yourself much more good if, instead of saying your prayers, you teach yourself to adjust your 'linguistic diarrhea' as I call it - your inner monologue, the way you talk to yourself. If you can learn to control those words and thoughts of yours, you could do and be so much more. Many people believe in the power of prayers, believing that whatever they pray for will become a reality. In this same way, you can 'pray' to your own spirit and strengthen your own self-believe system. Try saying to yourself every day for a month that those jeans look amazing on you and BELIEVE it. Then notice how people start looking at you more, and giving you compliments every time you wear those jeans ☺

You can find 'controlling' tendencies in every religion. There is a brilliant story to illustrate that, the story of a Russian Tzar who decided to unite and control the masses in his kingdom through one religion. Eventually he decided that the three religions which appealed to him the most were Christianity, Buddhism and Islam.

It is said that the only reason he turned down the other religions in favour of Christianity for a simple reason: the others would not allow him and his people to drink vodka.

Please understand, I am not criticizing or questioning the heritage of any religion. I am simply raising the idea that we are constantly evolving. Are the old religions serving your needs now? Are you full of joy 24/7? Are you completely free of fear? Have you found internal peace? If not then maybe, just maybe, you should start looking for the things you seek within yourself.

Once, as humans, we had learned how to sustain ourselves physically and keep the wolf (or the bear... or the other threats out there) from the door, then we started developing further by becoming more human and less animal. We started to evolve further, emotionally and intellectually. Then, our ego kicked in. And ego doesn't have to be a bad thing. It really is a good thing to possess, as it protects us in a way and makes us each unique.

If you pay close attention, most of the main religions were formed when land wars were quite a common occurrence. People were in constant conflict, and there was hardly any order. Order is what is needed for progress.

Religion played a key role in uniting people to a common cause, and provided the human race with that sense of security that we crave so deeply.

Religion also made people feel special, and separated humans from the animals. So who am I to blame people for following it? However, as humans have developed further and become who we are today, I believe that now is the time to recognise a new age: An age of creativity and individuality, giving you the chance to share your own internal truth (something you may well still need to discover).

You are a fully developed but also constantly-evolving human being who is unique to our life as we know it. You are so lucky to live at this time of true individuality. Now is YOUR time.

Celebrating being a human being is no longer about 'help' and being 'saved'. How can you possibly 'help' others, how can you possibly save the world? The world does not need to be saved. Life is now about your experiences, and something that I call a 'creative process' - what you, as a unique individual, can contribute to the world. It is about your personal knowledge and the strength that you can offer. Not by helping others, but by articulating your talents. It is as simple as that.

It is not as easy though as it sounds. You are on the verge of major change and evolution and you are still bound by old beliefs and old traditions. It is difficult to break free of such emotional commitments. Yet in order to progress and experience truly enlightening changes, you really need to move yourself forward first.

You can do this by understanding and accepting what life is about - constant development. We can experience this by simply watching the beautiful soft clouds peacefully floating in the sky or watching children play. Yet, this is not all the joys life has to offer. I am referring to the current and the future. You'll never really know the complete answers to everything in life. And how can you? It is ever-evolving! Life is never still.

You can't possibly know the answers to something has not happened yet. You can only predict what might happen based on past experiences. As those adverts for financial products love to say in the small print: Past results may not reflect future results. Your actions can have unintended consequences. What about the co-creative process? When you combine your actions with the actions of another human being? Look at Apple, for example. It wasn't just Steve Jobs who created the iphone. It was the co-creative process of hundreds of people working with Mr Jobs that produced one of the most desirable gadgets of all time.

That is the very beauty of it. You are not secure. You can't possibly be. You are simply experiencing life and enjoying living it (even if you aren't enjoying it now... but I hope you will be soon!) while testing the new possibilities and opportunities that are open to you. By observing the results of your experiences and co-creations you can really learn to make the most of who you are and understand what can be achieved if you work with others. You might be an amazing artist, for example, but if you're a crap salesperson, it's possible that no one will see your works - simply because they are not on display at the right time and the right place. That is a very simplistic explanation of co-creative process, but at least you get the idea. Make sure that your old beliefs don't hold you back anymore.

One of the main challenges in life is to break free of these imposed beliefs. We are creatures of habit. Whether these habits are right or wrong, we know them. We know how to go about them. At this point I'm going to simply ask you to remember your childhood, not the sad moments, but the moments you were chasing a dragonfly without worrying it might harm you, or tasting a new food for the first time and suddenly discovering you really like it. You just never know what might be out there, offering you even more joy and happiness... maybe even love.

I travel a lot and no matter where I am people are always full of questions: Why? What does it all mean? Why am I in pain? Who can help me?

The truth is that you have no understanding of what life is, and in many ways you never will. Life is ever-evolving. You are the creator and a unique and rare soul. Please understand that it is not so much about having all the answers – it's about the wisdom and knowledge you personally acquire while you experiment with life.

Your perception is completely unique to you, which means that every single experience is unique to you too.

The key thing to remember is that we never stop evolving. Remember that life and YOU are not staying still, you are either progressing or regressing. Which one will you choose?

So matter what you've done, no matter what you have experienced so far, now is the time for you to start transferring what others have told you into a true belief in yourself.

I'm sure you are working through certain emotions or dealing with certain events and disappointments, but it isn't this that is holding you back. It is your unchanged state of mind that puts you back into the hamster wheel, time and time again. It is not always about success. You may need to experience failure in order to learn and build your own personal knowledge.

If you're constantly striving for perfection and running on that wheel, it could lead to feelings of stress, anxiousness or even depression.

You are not making the same mistakes over and over because of karma, your past wrongdoings or whatever else your religion might tell you. Karma is an invented word. Invented by humans to keep the 'excuse' running so they do not feel responsible for themselves. Yes, it is scary at first, to take your first step towards claiming responsibility, but once you start, you will realise that it's hugely empowering.

Yes, you will fail and probably more than once! How many times did you keep failing when you were learning to walk as a child? How many words of encouragement did it take from your parents or those who looked after you before you actually started WALKING? This time you won't have as much encouragement, because you are a grown up now... but that's why you need to build your own internal support system, your own encouragement 'tape'. And once you do succeed, you'll be empowered for the rest of your life. That victory is going to be yours and yours only. That joy of succeeding on your own is one of the most wonderful feelings in the world.

In a way, karma is like someone who deliberately tries to make you responsible for their emotional satisfaction, and makes you feel guilty if you don't succeed. If you believe in karma, you are that person's victim. However, if you do believe you are in control of your actions and the situations you'll attract, then you will understand that karma is meaningless. By adjusting your feelings, emotions and actions accordingly you will see that it is possible to change your life for yourself.

Your beautiful body

Most of us fail to love our bodies and accept them exactly the way they are. Or sometimes we need to relearn body acceptance and love after surgeries or other major physical events.

It took me two major surgical operations before I understood there is no point in fighting and hiding my scars. I've learnt to keep them as a reminder of certain actions I no longer want to repeat and I've learnt to love every bit of my body, even the parts I think are 'ugly'. Everyone has parts they love or hate.

It doesn't matter what you think, there always will be someone who thinks of you as the most beautiful person in the world. Why not start with yourself? Why not be the first to fall in love with your very own body as it is right now. Deformed or not. Perfect or not. With scars or not. Projected emotions are a very powerful tool.

Many people have an issue with their body. Some go further, and transfer their body issues into everyday life. They do everything possible to change their bodies, including plastic surgery and some try as much as possible to ignore parts of their body completely by covering them up. Baggy clothes anyone? Or an extra large flower or piece of jewellery, or a how about a hat?

I've had many experiences with this. At times, in hospital after a complex operation or a long recovery, when I could not move at all and the stitches were only just removed, I'd look at my body as if it was some foreign object and not mine at all.

When I was going through my (unsuccessful) IVF treatment, I had such a major reaction to it that the doctors were seriously scared for my life. As a result of the amount of medication needed to save me, once I started to recover, I noticed the body I now had was not mine at all.

It was mine all right, but the changes it went through so suddenly left me with a severely distorted and overweight body instead of my regular well-trimmed self. When I realized what had happened, I was in such shock I was literally running from myself. I wanted nothing to do with me. I'd go for extra long walks, avoiding any human being. I'd avoid mirrors. I stopped wearing my much-loved clothes.

While my transformation was rather dramatic, this phenomenon is not limited to those who've had traumatic medical experiences.

I've worked with many people whose appearance is completely normal - if 'normal' exists – yet they've experienced the same attitude towards their body. I'm sure you've experienced this yourself. Looking at your skin or your face in the mirror, maybe your hair is really bedraggled, and you think, me? Is that me? Why do I look like that? Why do I not have a face like my friend, or that movie actor? Surely one time or another, you have felt that your body is a foreign object, or that you hate some part of it.

This happens because you are a spiritual being first of all and a physical being secondly. Yes, you are not just a social animal. You have a mind, and you have a soul. Your body is something temporary. It is a bit like you car. Treat it badly, it'll break down. Constantly ignore the repairs the car badly needs, and it will stop running.

If you eat particular foods your (and I really want to focus on the word your) body does not like, ask any car mechanic and they'll explain to you what happens when you put diesel inside a Bugatti. It does not like it. Your body will not like it. It'll break down eventually.

There is no need to hate something which helps you to live your life, no matter what traits you've inherited. Yes, you may have an extra long nose or a really dry skin or it may be that your hair grows everywhere or you are severely overweight.

Whatever shape your precious body is, you better start treating it as your 'transport' in this life. You can't move in our physical world as you know it without it.

So why don't you love it? Why don't you appreciate the work it does for you, even if it is as trivial as your hands and fingers delivering food into your mouth.

Even if it is to thank your tongue for moving fast enough and dexterously enough to help you pronounce sounds and talk to your friends and family. You can do nothing in this life without your body. Treat it gently and kindly. Love it and appreciate it. Thank it. Do what it wants of you. Find physical exercise you enjoy rather than ones you feel you should do. If your body hates running, don't run. If it loves dancing, dance. Just be kind to your poor body, and it will be kinder to you.

About food… I am not a nutritionist, but one thing I can say for sure. Be aware that what's a good food or a good diet for one person, may be terrible food for you. How do you find out? By listening to your body.

I'll give you a very small exercise for now just to get you started, and that may well be the only thing you'll ever need.

But most importantly, you do need to start listening to your body. I've been working with a girl who spends her life constantly on a diet and consuming nothing but chamomile tea, yet she does nothing but increase in size.

Your mind is the biggest influence on your body. Whenever I get carried away by reading fashion magazines and seeing some new diet or other being promoted, I try to remember that I may actually gain weight by following them rather than lose any. Not because that diet is wrong or bad, it may be quite the opposite and is really getting great results for SOME people, but it may not necessarily produce the same results for me. At the same time whenever I eat whatever my heart desires, it seems than no matter how much I eat, I do not manage to gain a single gram.

Here's that exercise I was talking about...

Simply stay still for five minutes or so a day, close your eyes, concentrate on your body, and ask whether it needs anything of you.

Is there a particular vitamin or a food it desires in order to be healthier or fitter?

Then simply wait. One day you'll notice you have a craving for a tomato, another day you'll feel like eating some fruit even if you rarely eat fruit, and so on. A few months down the line, this will happen automatically. You'll feel a need to consume a particular food at the time that's right for you.

Just try it. How does it feel? What happens? Experiment! You might just be delighted with what follows and how you feel after doing that for a while.

Another issue linked to our hatred for our bodies is self-harm. On this topic, I want to talk about my own story, and then I'll sum up the stories of a few of my clients.

By the way, all my clients are pretty normal! Although I suppose, 'normal' is the wrong word, for there is no such thing. But they are very successful people, even if they've been through personal troubles and needed my help. They are regular people, with pluses and minuses just like all of us. They work, or they run their own businesses.

They're usually very attractive and the majority have gone through several relationships by the time they come to me. You would never in a million years guess the emotional pain they deal with.

The reason I mention this is that you can be critical of yourself and sometimes you may feel you are not normal, that there's something wrong with you.

There isn't. You are a unique human being with a strong spirit – that is why you are here and not dead! Just living requires a lot of mental and of spiritual strength. Give yourself credit for it.

It may well be that you are going through the same pain I went through because you feel like you are missing some answers to important questions. Or maybe you are using any opportunity to distract yourself from uncomfortable thoughts or emotional pain by projecting that pain onto your body. Or it may be you thought you were abnormal, and you wanted to make yourself feel more special.

No. You are already truly astonishing. You've listened to others for too long, you have listened to the news for too long, you've read magazines for too long, you've been watching movies for too long, you've been with your family for too long.

You've imprinted their beliefs and their ideas onto your precious brain and with time you've forgotten to ask yourself what you really think, and who you really are.

You became a slave to whoever has influenced your mind throughout your life so far. It is time to break these chains.

Back to self-harm. There is nothing worse you can do than to hurt your body. I know. I've been there and I understand you. Some of my clients have shared some self-harming stories which will make your hair not only stand up, but will make you jump right out of your body! The most commonly shared tale was similar to mine. I'm sharing it here for the first time. Even my parents do not know. . I've hidden my scars very well.

The minute we feel as though we lose control, we want to punish ourselves for being so weak, and we hurt our bodies. Some cut themselves, some bite themselves, some try to inflict hurt themselves in more subtle ways – with risky behaviour, most commonly alcohol, or whatever your 'poison' is.

But by hurting ourselves, we do not prove anything to anyone. We do not increase control over anything. We simply hurt, ruin and destroy the very 'vehicle' that allows us to live and experience our own lives.

I've met many people in my life who later took their own lives. Sadly, you probably know at least one person who's done the same thing, or tried to.

I know of so many people who believe they are weak and can't face their life any more. There is nothing worse you can do. It is like killing a person who cannot protect themselves. You are defenseless. (Unless you fight back in your mind and decide to take another way – please, please do preserve your unique life!)

If you believe that by dying, you'll force people around you to miss you and regret not being nicer to you - it doesn't quite work like that. They might grieve for you in the beginning, but then they go on with their lives, and rightly so. You do not prove anything with your death but the weakness of your character and disrespect for the life you've come on earth to live. You can only make a statement by living - by experiencing, creating, and by taking a control of your life's direction. Death is saying nothing. It's silence, forever.

Wouldn't you rather express yourself with your living, breathing body, and your words?

Your body is your temple. It should come first.

Not your church. Not your house. Not your family. All of those things come after.

Your body comes first. Your body is your temple where the work and actions of your mind and soul start to become possible. Treat your body as the holiest temple in the world. Thank it for the opportunities it gives you to turn your thoughts into reality. Treasure your body for letting you move around and eat and feel the breeze on your skin, actions which translate into emotions of pleasure, serenity and astonishment. This all is unique to us human beings, thanks to the body we have been born with. Love it and treasure it.

Now, start giving it the treatment it deserves. Bathe it, polish it, exercise it, and give it praise. Fall in love with it. You may not like your feet, but you are definitely grateful for the opportunity to walk. You may not be happy with your nose, but you are definitely grateful for the opportunity to smell the flowers.

Once you fall in love with your body you will find the beauty in it that's been there all along. It may be that you have particularly beautiful fingers, or it may be that your skin feels particularly soft this morning. Perhaps you've been complimented on your eyes or your hair.

Thank each of these parts of your body and fall in love with them. Your body will respond to this. One day you'll realize what a beautiful pair of ears you have. The next month you'll see your waist has slimmed down a tiny bit should you crave to have a slimmer self, and you will be grateful to your body for responding to the shape you'd rather it be.

It does take time. Eventually your body will respond. After all, it probably took you at least five years to get your body to its current shape. Give it some credit and it will pay you back beyond your wildest dreams and expectations.

Picture a little puppy that seems to be lost and abandoned and lies half dead in the middle of the road. You want to save it, right? That is your body. Save it. Love it. Care for it. It will reward you with more than you thought possible. It's your temple, it's your altar. It's also temporary. Learn to love it and appreciate it while you have it.

Money

'Money, it turned out, was exactly like sex, you thought of nothing else if you didn't have it and thought of other things if you did.'

James Baldwin

Many years ago, our great great great......great grandparents were either harvesting fruits, rearing cattle, or growing grain. When they needed something they did not make themselves, they would go to a neighbour who was happy to exchange potatoes for meat, or fruit for cloth.

If you needed a particular medicine, you might need to do several exchanges like this before you'd get what you needed. You would have to trade what you had multiple times in order to acquire what you wanted. Certain goods were transported for many days and weeks and months before they could be exchange for silk or spices or guns or jewels.

Slowly the goods in higher demand where introduced as a currency, so produce would be exchanged for salt, spice, jewels etc. And that slowly morphed into one valuable commodity: Gold. Which then became money.

Money has saved you the trouble of finding out who produces the bread you want to buy and what they want to trade for it. It's saved you from long journeys, from multiple exchanges, from the temporary nature of goods like fruits that might rot before they could be traded.

Money is the bridge between your work and the goods you want to own or you believe are necessary to make your life more enjoyable. Imagine for example working for a publishing company and earning in books - how would you exchange them, should you have an urge to eat for example? How would you establish who needs these books, and more importantly that they also have the product or the food you are after? So money is your friend, because the creation of money has saved you enormous amounts of time and energy, which you can now spend on your own life.

So why do you criticize money? It really does not make any sense to blame money for your problems. It is not a living human being, and you are. Money serves you and works very hard for you, but decisions relating to money are all yours. I love hearing people say 'money is the root of all evil'. That just makes me laugh every time. It is as if they openly and loudly announce: 'I am an idiot, and I have failed to live and co-exist with other human beings!' Rather than recognizing that (in some cases) you want to have more than you need – it is easier to blame something or someone.

The only reason you are short of money (at least on a temporary basis) is you. Let me rephrase – it's your own fault. Yes, it is possible that you were born into the poor family. Yes, it is possible that you, for one reason or another, may be struggling financially. And yes, while temporarily you may feel as though life is unfair to you, once your situation is emotionally worked through you may actually find the power inside you to make different choices. Those choices will lead to different results. This is the case in every aspect of your life, and money is no different.

Of course there are circumstances we simply cannot prepare ourselves for. When my husband died, our papers were not in order and as a result my finances were under threat. While grieving, I also had to deal with the questions in my head - 'Why did you abandon me and why would you put me in such difficult financial situation?'. Later, I saw the cause of my misfortune was my own ignorance. I did what everyone does: I simply spent less energy and stayed lazy. It was easier at the time to make my husband responsible for my investments. So I didn't learn for myself how to look after my own money.

Of course there are circumstances that affect your financial life. But that is what life is. You can't possibly prepare yourself for absolutely everything, you can try, but then you'll spend your whole life doing just that: preparing.

You can also get rid of everything and go with the flow (i.e. making everything as you go), but than you are denying your very purpose here. Life is evolving because of your participation in it! If you need to constantly work to make ends meet, then how will you share that internal creativity with others? How will you find the time to share your emotional happiness with others? You may love doing something which brings you money, in which case, my congratulations on being able to put the two together. For the rest of you, let's just start somewhere in order to improve the situation, so that you can put yourself into the mentality of 'having more than enough'. Money is not the root of all evil. Your uncontrollable desires are. Should you feel you are short of money, then start by learning to control your cravings, even just temporarily.

There is absolutely nothing wrong with having too much money and spending it as you wish. It is however ridiculously wrong to be jealous of someone who has more money than you do. This may be because you are being too lazy to really challenge yourself, instead finding it easier to blame the world around you for your lack of funds. That is always the simplest path, staying lazy and blaming others. It is convenient to blame something which can't speak for itself, isn't it?

Your world around you is mainly (not 100 percent, but mainly) the direct result of your own actions and your co-creative processes with other humans. Money is good in many ways. It's a tool - money helps you do a specialized job. Money is not responsible for your actions.

Time and again my clients say to me: 'All I want is to provide for my kids and be able stop saying 'we can't afford this', I just want to have a decent flat and a car which doesn't break down.'

Materialistic? Not at all. You do need to satisfy your basic needs – and even some of your less basic ones - in order to keep your brain free for more creative processes.

However, our needs are all different. Should you be the hippy who only needs a slice of bread and a glass of water a day, that's your choice – but you have no right to use it to make yourself feel better than the person who want to provide for his kids or take his wife on luxurious holidays.

Needs and desires are different depending on each individual person, and that is what makes our earthly community so unique. Life can't stay still - it's against physics! So, if it's got to move, it's your choice – it either goes backwards or forwards. It gets better or it gets worse.

Which would you rather?

As I write this chapter, it's the summer of 2011 and the riots are breaking and London is, quite literally, burning.

Sadly the timing of what I want to say here couldn't be any better. Emotions are not as intangible as you think them to be. They are very much physical things, and what's even more important to acknowledge is that our emotions are contagious.

Ever entered a room full of ill or wounded people? Did you feel particularly happy and cheerful? Or ever entered a party with lots of smiling people and immediately feel like you wanted to be part of their joy?

That's because every day you pick up other people's emotions. Whether good or bad. And in a similar way, your emotions may transmit to others. The higher the number of people contaminated with a particular idea, the more difficult it is to resist joining them.

Here is just one witness to the riots:

"The looters were yelling at us to get down and throwing stuff all over the place. I got down and started taking off my wedding and engagement ring to hide somewhere, but unfortunately wasn't fast enough. One looter came up and demanded my phone. I didn't have it with me since it was in my purse and it was out of arm reach. I also didn't want to lead him to my passport, so I said I didn't have one.

He told me to take off my rings and grabbed my hand, trying to yank them off. His friend tried to help too, but the rings wouldn't come off and I just yelled at him that I'd take them off myself. In hindsight, now that I know that gun control is so fierce in England and he only had a bat, I should have held on to my rings better and maybe slugged him in the face."

What you are not aware of is that, whether you are trying to save the world or simply deal with your bad-mannered relative, you possess a great power. Often people have no idea of this. It's the power of your own emotions. Most people do not realize you can choose an emotion depending on the outcome you seek. Your ability to control or change your emotions at any given time will impact on your relationship with others.

Have you ever had one of those dates when you meet someone and start hitting it off at once? You finish each other's sentences, your interests are the same and the next thing you know you have all the same opinions.

Are you really interested in the same things? Or might it be that one mind influences another? Could you be coming together and meeting in the middle, subtly shifting your behaviour so that you can be closer?

Humans do this all the time, and emotions are acting as transmitters. Excitement, fear, uncertainty or guilt – they're very contagious, transmitted easily from one human 'host' to another. But they also 'infect' your actions. An example:

Let's consider 'uncertainty':

Whenever I am working on achieving any goal, be that to write a book or to create a workshop, I always get that feeling of uncertainty. I start doubting myself. I want to know for a fact that I'll succeed. I do not want to waste my time and have things go pear-shaped down the line.

Interestingly, looking back now, when I used to run my lingerie business I had no chance to have an emotion like 'uncertainty'. The business was simply something I loved doing at that time and produced an income I could not have dreamt of previously. So there was no time to even think whether I was even good enough.

It is surprising how with age and experience some people may become more uncertain, rather than less. They (and myself at times) forget that it is the experience itself that matters, not our success.

Perhaps it is that as we get older, we tend to have more responsibilities, more people we believe are depending on us. Thus we tend to listen to others' needs more and we become more cautious.

The faster you accept there are no absolute answers to anything, the easier it will be develop into the person you want to be – the 'God' of your own life, if you like, living in the temple of your body. J I like that image! It tickles me.

If you didn't receive the bonus you were so waiting for and now you can't buy that present for your wife, or if you lost your job and now you can't afford to take your child to the zoo – this isn't the end of the world. But the emotions and the guilt such events evoke in you are beyond what is rational.

Anxiety kicks in and self-worth is taken away, and soon you are afraid that your wife will leave you, that your children will be homeless. The more doubts enter your mind, the more they will materialize to support your thoughts, because your attention shifts and shifts to the very direction you are trying to avoid. Once such stability is broken, it can take years to re-build.

My father's hair went grey overnight after his business was confiscated by the Latvians once the country got its independence from the USSR. They did it because he was Russian and because they could. He has never quite recovered. He puts his brave face on and continues living on to support his family, but he has never quite recovered. How many people like that do you know?

What we fail to understand is that everything in this life is temporary. Everything changes, all the time, and you can't stop that.

We try to hang on to things, and that's not surprising. Anything that helps us sustain our body and our sanity it is worth trying to hold on to. But once you accept that nothing is permanent it'll be easier for you to deal with loss and find new delights to replace the lost things. The same is true with uncertainty: once you accept you will never know the absolute answers, you don't need to worry so much about not knowing them.

And, let's be clear, you cannot know.

There has never been any human being like you ever before, with the same exact life experience as yours, going for this venture you are trying, be that your business, be that your hobby, or any major goal. You cannot know the answer to something you are about to create. Your life is ART. I'm guessing you do not want your life to be a forgery. And guess what, you cannot be a forgery, no matter how hard you try, for you are absolutely unique. There is simply no other like you.

If you believe in yourself, and if you expect success, you are more likely to achieve it.

During some major changes in my life, I was working with a psychic who came to me as a client. Out of curiosity and because I was faced with events that I found it difficult to explain, I decided to ask her some questions and find out what she had to say. She gave me some predictions regarding my work and personal relationships. I didn't entirely like what I heard, and while I accepted what she said, I also wanted to challenge her statements.

Since her predictions for the timing of a particular event seemed to me to be much too optimistic, so I went home and adjusted my actions and emotions. Then I went to see her a month later. She looked amused and she gave me a different date, significantly earlier than the one she had given me previously!

Whether she was right or wrong, I honestly don't know. Some of the information she gave me was absolutely correct and true, and she had no way of knowing these things.

Yet I then made so many deliberate changes in my life that some of the things she told me were no longer relevant. The point I am making here is that even if psychics can predict the future, we are still in control; we can change and adjust events to our liking.

While we can never control absolutely everything, as other people's lives are interacting with and influencing ours, we can often control more than we think.

When people are in search of answers, they tend to believe what they want to hear. They do not realize they've fallen into the 'belief' trap and that it is they themselves make the predictions come true by their actions.

The future will hold for you whatever you want it to hold, depending on your belief in yourself. With this in mind, I grab myself in my mind's eye and continue writing this book - because I am just like you, and doubts try to creep into my mind. If I believe this book will get written, it will get written, dammit!

And look, here it is, in your hands. ☺

So here is a mantra for you:

'I have no clue how I succeed at _____ (write your goal) but I know I will succeed!'

Full stop.

Say that to yourself every day (with the gap filled in, obviously). How does it make you feel? You might find yourself doing something 'impossible' before very long. Believe you can do it, and you will. 'How' will look after itself. 'How' is just the details!

Here's something I've learned. Perhaps you can test it for yourself.

There is no such thing as changing the world by trying to change the world. You can only change yourself.

Your emotions influence others. They'll join in. Others always do, because emotions are so catchy, like a song or like a disease. But the change starts from you - your thoughts and your actions - not by trying to persuade someone to do something. Persuasion meets resistance and the need to justify. When you behave, act, and do what you believe is great, others will have no choice but to join in. As an old folk tale once described it: 'monkey see, monkey do'! We're not monkeys, but when we're in groups, we can behave shockingly like them sometimes.

There are many of us who want to be part of something. I want to be part of someone else's life. I want to be part of my friends' circle. We are social animals and we long to belong.

The paradox is we also want to be unique and stand out while at the same time yearning to be accepted. So we shop for the best, eat at the best restaurants, try to be more creative than others. There is no need to do that. Only do what pleases you (as long as it doesn't damage others), and the rest follow.

Here's an example. You are meeting some friends for dinner, but you decide in advance you're not going to drink tonight. But once you get there, everyone else decides to share a bottle of wine and your resolve crumbles. You join in.

As I mentioned earlier, the streets of London are currently burning in the aftermath of the riots. My Greek mother (my deceased husband's mother) lives in a special building for elderly people. Just few nights ago the rioters lit the residents' cars on fire, they lit building's garden on fire, and they began running through the building with petrol canisters, shouting that they were going to burn the residents alive.

Luckily the police arrived just in time, my mum was ok and I hope that the other residents didn't have any harmful spikes in their blood pressure. But what were these rioters thinking? Did they really need to burn elderly people alive? Obviously not. They were emotionally contaminated by the other rioters' emotions. They weren't quite themselves – the emotions took over. Don't be like the rioters, have your own mind and choose your own path!

You can observe this emotional contamination in everyday life too. You've seen the same TV advert about a particular snack many times, but you insist you will not get hooked. Then your friend tells you she can't get hold of the snack as it has become so popular, and the next thing you know you are intrigued. The next time you see the snack in the shop, you'll probably get it.

Or you are meeting a close friend for a drink she tells you about a horrible new person in her office. Then you go out and meet a few of her co-workers and they all mention horrible things about this new person. Next month you go to their work party and you are introduced to the person everyone dislikes. You'll dislike him too, most probably, and now in conversation with him your brain will only register the information he supplies you with to confirm your 'bad' opinion of him. You were contaminated by emotions of others regarding this person.

Why is it important that emotions have such power? Because you have this magnificent power at your disposal if you choose to use it! And you constantly contaminate or are contaminated by others' emotions, whether you want to or not.

Unfortunately, you are probably already contaminated, because if you knew you had such power in your hands you would not listen for hours to your moaning friend and then feel grumpy for the rest of the day. You would avoid watching movies that make you feel depressed or angry. I have to admit that I sometimes watch movies like that just so that I can experience the emotions my clients go through. Of course I've been through all of them before, but now that I've grown aware of their power I am a little bit better at controlling them.

So how do you start making use of such powers? Let's start with the basics. If you want anyone to respect you, start respecting yourself. Find a way to respect just one aspect of yourself, no matter how small it is. You'll slowly notice there are more aspects of yourself you can respect. It's only a matter of time before you start noticing how others have started respecting you.

You want to be loved? Start loving yourself. Love is an emotion. Emotion is contagious. People will have no choice but to fall in love with you. Sounds ridiculous? Try it. Experiment.

You want other people to join your project? Guess what. Fall in love with it. Believe in it. You'll attract people who will fall in love with it too. Because you can contaminate them emotionally.

You may not necessarily 'contaminate' the people you target, for you never have control over another human being! Nor should you. But your emotions will contaminate others and probably those most easily affected will be the ones who are drawn to a similar idea. More people will follow. That's the way emotions work.

You feel afraid. Find the strength not to be afraid of something, and the look in your eyes will adjust ever so slightly, which will help you to push away the things that scare you. That will give you more assurance, you'll feel less afraid, and less scary stuff will come to your life. So what is it exactly that you are afraid of?

In order to be better in control of yourself and to stop others imposing their emotions on you, you must work to achieve total liberation from imposed opinions and boundaries. That is the place to start if you want to center yourself and start re-discovering yourself. Once you have mastered this, it will help you to recognize the very life purpose you seek, or what many call 'enlightenment'.

Childhood pain

We all went through some sort of trauma as children. It might be physical pain or emotional abuse, your parents or a school bully, or something truly horrendous that no living creature should have to go through. The truth is, you are no longer going through that trauma.

Most likely, that experience has taught you something while also damaging you in many other ways, and that damage is now blocking you from enjoying your life completely. You can choose to react to that trauma from a different angle. It is no longer happening. You can choose to acknowledge that it is no longer part of your life. In this new life you can choose which direction and actions you take. In this new life, as from NOW, you are in total control. You do not let your memory control you – you can control your memory. You don't need to change your life, you simply want to live it differently.

The easiest way to move forward is to acknowledge that whatever it is you went through is a pool of knowledge you can draw upon - nothing more. Every step in your day is a new step, every morning you awake to a new morning. This is true of any trauma, not just a childhood trauma. Yes, you may still have financial problems, or your partner has still left you, or you still know that nothing will bring your child back, but you also realize it is a brand new day.

Every moment is a brand new moment. There are new actions you can take and there are new thoughts you can think, new emotions you can experience and new opportunities to take advantage of. Any moment, new and amazing people might appear in your life. As from TODAY, everything is as you want it to be, starting from your thoughts, your imagination, and your choices.

Do remember you still have a body to look after and manage. If you dramatically change your life, your body may suffer. And with change comes uncertainty. Some people feel sudden mood swings and almost depression. That is your 'body memory' trying to get you back to its usual routines and states.

I lived with a drug addict for a while and though he took many drugs, it was marijuana that seemed to be the most difficult habit to break. Every time we fought with his habit, he started getting mood swings and became nervous and aggressive. Years later I spoke to a friend whose husband smokes non-stop and she admitted it was easier for her to accept him smoking than try to help him quit, for the mood swings, the irritation and the aggression were unbearable. The body will fight back, so be prepared.

Ever tried to lose weight fast? Remember those cravings and the sudden urges to eat anything and everything in your way? Remember comforting yourself that you've lost enough and saying that you'll be back on the diet again from tomorrow?

Smaller changes are better, but you have to start training your willpower as soon as possible. Any changes must start with your willingness, the more you are willing, the easier it will be to stay in control. You can train your willpower on small things and then once you feel you are ready you can test your willpower on bigger things. Changes require emotional strain from you.

An amazing client came to me to deal with a relationship issue, but what struck me about her was the fact that for no reason whatsoever she had stopped eating chocolate. She happily admitted she had no need to stop eating one of her favourite foods - she was slim and had a really striking figure. But she felt that she was not able to control anything in her life, so experimented with herself to see if she could stop eating chocolate. She eventually succeeded. I know many may not agree with her choosing chocolate as her starting point! But choosing a starting point will help you. It may be that you need to start going to the gym regularly, for example only once a week, but definitely every week. The choice is yours, sticking to your goals is what is important here.

Later, the same client decided to stop eating cheese, another of her favourite foods. Please note, she still ate a lot, it was never about her weight, it was about learning to deny herself the 'substance' she loves so much. A few months after that, she had built up enough self-belief to stay in control, and she was able to break free of a very emotionally abusive relationship where she really loved the guy. By starting with small things, she was able to realize she had the power to escape that relationship.

Isn't it amazing to have the opportunity to talk to almost anyone you want, at the touch of a button? Or how about simply connecting with a remote holiday resort and asking them for a recommendation of what to pack for your trip? How about selling your business services to people who are so far away that not only do they not speak your language, they've never even heard of the place where you're based?

You are probably familiar with Tourism Queensland's groundbreaking, 'The Best Job in the World' campaign, which was a PR and viral marketing phenomenon that generated worldwide media attention.

The concept was simple: post a one-minute video application on Tourism Queensland's website explaining why you should be chosen as the caretaker of Hamilton Island on the Great Barrier Reef, and you might get to blog and cam your way through a six-month gig that paid about $100,000 U.S.

The story broke with a Reuters placement (advertising) around sunrise in Australia on January 12, 2009. By breakfast time in London, Associated Press was interviewing Tourism Queenslands's UK director for a broadcast package that turned up on the morning shows in the U.S. As a result within just two days there were 1,100 TV placements in the U.S alone. In just 30 hours they had 400,000 new visitors, when their original goal had been to get that number over the course of the whole one-year campaign!

Or how about online dating sites? They have such a high rate of success that many people only consider online dating nowadays. And why wouldn't they? I mean, once you are out of the education system, your chances of meeting new people can be somewhat limited. Obviously for some people, online dating sites can seem a bit like romantic shopping lists - but wait till you read a bit further.

One of my clients is an amazing jeweller at DeBeers. Her workshop is in the basement and she spends most of her day alone. During her spare time she works on her own business. All of this has left her with very limited social exposure. She simply did not meet enough new people. If you live alone or you are a single parent, the chance you'll find some free time to socialize is close to zero. And even if you do, your energy level is often too limited to present yourself in the best possible way. For these people, online dating is the perfect solution.

Well, there you go. Social media is great, right? ☺

These days many of my friends do not leave their house without an ipad or any other device which keeps them online 24/7 and they keep checking for their twitter and facebook or other social-media outlet updates. Isn't it amazing?! Just when we thought we were all becoming robots, we've got those amazing devices, which make us more human. We communicate MORE!

NOW WAIT... DO WE? I mean, do we communicate more? The last time I checked the meaning of 'communication' it stated: 'common possession, sharing; fellowship; an emotional bond with' and so on. We seem to meet all the requirements via social media at the first glance, don't we?

There is one key thing that we are forgetting, and that is when you communicate via the internet the other person can only see your words and only guess at the emotions that come with them. Partially due to our ego and partially due to the ease of talking in this way, we can sometimes interpret what someone else is saying in the way we want to. This can lead to huge misinterpretations and misunderstandings.

There is also the language issue. Many languages, some more than others, have several meanings attached to singular words. I will never forget how frustrating it was for me discovering that in order to explain one thing in English I had to use a word that already meant different things to me.

I mean, the English language may seem relatively simple, but if it's not spoken in person, words it can mean very different things in different situations.

I suppose this is the root of the famous British sense of humour:

-'Basil!'

-'Coming, my little piranha fish.'

Sybil and Basil Fawlty, Fawlty Towers.

Secondly, an essential part of being human is to use our whole body in order to communicate, i.e. body language, facial expressions, intonation and even the volume of our voices. You've probably had an experience where you really hit it off with someone via the internet, and then you meet in person and… the person is nothing like how you imagined they would be. Not always, because you might not even end up meeting everyone you speak to on social media. That isn't always the purpose of talking to them in the first place.

Guess what? It is not the other person's problem that you see them in a different light (unless, as my friend who used online dating politely put it, 'it is really difficult to hide when you state you are 6 foot tall and in reality you are barely 5'4') But it isn't entirely your fault either. When only typed words are used as a communication, huge amounts of missing information will be filled in via assumption.

How about the opportunity to be who you want to be? I mean, who can really see you when you're online? Or check whether what you say is really the truth?

I loved that scene in the movie 'Surrogates' (about robots who could be completely controlled via thought, which allowed humans to stay at home and live their lives via their robots) where Tom Greer played by Willis said:

"Honey, I don't know what you are. I mean, for all I know, you could be some big, fat dude sitting in his chair with his dick hanging out."

It's almost like role playing, letting you try out being another person. Just imagine, there is a whole world out there which you access via this tiny box in front of you and you are free to post any photo you want and any information you desire about yourself.

You know you can't change your face or your clothes but… why even bother getting dressed, when you can just sit with your messed up hair in clothes you haven't washed for a while or possibly even naked while lying in bed… and pretend you are whoever you actually want to be.

There are a number of long-term complications that come with this attitude. Should we let this bother us now? For many people, social media is an escape. They may be restricted by 'evil' parents and unable to party with their friends, or maybe they are bullied at school, or even at work, and suffer from cripplingly low self-esteem.

We shouldn't really live like this, but simple everyday life can be a routine, a bore, a struggle for survival and…. here is a 'fantasy' world that we can access at the touch of a keyboard! Brilliant!

Or so it seems. Until the time comes when your bad habits come out, wrong words will be typed, suspicious names will be dropped. Lying is sooooo difficult. After a while, you need to be a really brilliant liar to remember absolutely everything you said previously.

In fact I used to date a man who couldn't lie even if he wanted to, he found it to be a difficult social skill. After some time together, I learnt how much easier it is not to lie, so it became difficult if I actually needed to tell a lie.

So for the majority of people, your 'old' self will creep in again and you may end up bitterly disappointed. Because rather than learning to understand and develop, you are running away and fighting with the world.

Next time you want to think of social media as the 'real' world, consider these words:

'You can't take something off the Internet – it's like taking pee out of a pool.'

Energy

You've probably experienced the feeling of enormous emptiness when a person you've spent lots of time with goes away. This might be because of a relationship break-up, or perhaps your daughter left to join the army, or your friends moved out of town. Or worst of all, when a spouse or a family member dies.

That is because whenever you interact with another person you exchange energy (this is easier to understand if you consider that your thoughts and emotions as well as feelings are all energy). It's almost as though you leave a 'footprint' in someone else's body. They keep a tiny part of you with them. And you keep a tiny part of them with you.

Think about how teenagers start to hang out with the cool kids and begin copying them, until one day you see a cool kid skulking on your sofa instead of your child... and you do not like it.

They've exchanged energies, so much so that they have forgotten their own core. As they've become friends with this group, they've lost a part of themselves.

Not all is lost and you can put yourself back together – re-energise yourself, if you like - but the period of emptiness will always be there when you part from someone. Sad or not, right or wrong, you will have a craving to re-unite, even if the person was horrible to you, even if the relationship was never meant to work for you. Part of you got lost.

You need to time to recuperate. Some, without knowing and understanding what has happened might struggle to re-unite energetically with themselves. They might try to hang onto the past, thinking that reconnecting with that person will make everything easier. The truth is that you've given too much of your energy to that particular person or event.

Any action you do, absolutely any, will leave an imprint on another person, a trace or a memory you might call it. There is no such thing as privacy in some ways. Absolutely every thought, every action, every move of yours will be imprinted.

You won't be able to move forward unless until you centre yourself and put your broken pieces together. You need to detach yourself until you start to feel contented again, and start to remember what is important to you. You need to relearn how to be spontaneous, free and simply enjoy being and enjoy being alive. You cannot possibly do this without recognizing that everyone has been in your life for a reason. You need to recognize that the people who have hurt you have also helped you to grow and develop.

Before you continue reading, please try to think of a few people who have hurt you in the past. This might be your former boyfriend or a girlfriend – pick one. This person might be one of your parents, or your brother or sister.

Each chosen person needs your undivided attention. Pick just one for now. Then write down everything you hate about that person, write down every single thing they've ever done to upset you, write down anything disturbing about your relationship with them that comes to mind. Keep writing until you can think of nothing else.

Now go through each event one by one, through every situation step by step and learn! Yes, learn what you've failed to recognize before. Learn now, why these events were necessary in order for you to develop as a person.

I mean it.

Then you need to acknowledge that all this time, you've missed the whole point, you've failed to understand why this event took place.

Now you need to write a letter of thanks to your chosen person tell them every single benefit you've picked up by experiencing the things they put you through. This might mean simply appreciating your new partner more or knowing that your parents made you stronger and more prepared for dealing with similar people in your life.

Some former clients have very generously donated some of their letters for your benefit, so that you can understand what I mean. Maybe you'll notice some things you've missed in your relationship with the people you are complaining about.

Here is a letter written by one of my former clients to her ex-boyfriend:

"Dear xxxxxxx

I am writing this letter to share with you the pain and hurt I felt in the last year of our relationship.

When you chose xxxxxx over me I felt betrayed and that the love and emotion invested in our five year relationship had meant nothing.

There were many times I felt I sacrificed part of my personality in an attempt to secure your happiness. I realise now that only you can be responsible for your happiness and our relationship was not able to "fix" the challenges you faced.

As a result I have realised that our relationship is not the relationship I choose. I realise I have gained strength in appreciating the qualities I'm looking for in a partner.

I deserve a partner who recognises my needs as well as his own. I choose a partner who desires me and makes me feel special, who is supportive and above all enjoys what life has to offer.

Without our time together I may never have fully realised all that I have to give in a relationship and all that I deserve. For this I thank you.

I wish you well and hope that you too can move forward and find happiness.

Grace."

Grace is not the only one. If each of us could write a similar letter and work out for ourselves what it is that we've learned from these experiences, it would create a calmness in our hearts and give us a deeper understanding of our own life. Grace is not alone. We all need to learn to appreciate the interactions we go through with other people, for better or for worse.

Here is a letter shared by my other client Georgina to her mother. Georgina has worked with me through the full five month program and while to the outside world, Georgina appears beautiful and successful, inside she had doubts and feelings of despair, and didn't know where to go for help. Just by following the ideas presented in this book, her life has changed dramatically. It all started with this letter to her mother.

It took a great deal of persuasion before she would let me share this with you, so please please treasure the opportunity to read it. It is one person's life, which may possibly relate to one or another aspect in your life. Here it is:

"Dear Mummy,

I wanted to write to you to let you know I think you are amazing. At times, our friendship is such that it is quite possibly enviable, in that very few mothers and daughters are so very 'real' with each other. This is seriously rare and something to be admired. However, without putting a negative upon this bond of ours, it has at times leaked into too familiar territory. Possible no definite border line between us. I do rely on you, your opinion, your strength of judgement and prejudices a lot. Actually an enormous amount and I believe through no-one's fault, purely a natural progression, possibly laziness, this has generated in me a weakness of my own opinions, very often. More often than not, I am not convinced of my convictions and so, feel a need to have another voice – someone else or indeed myself, question those opinions. Whether career, friends or a partner, I have never quite found my own feet. So much so, still at this age I have now reached, I am still not armed with a defined view of what or who truly makes me tick.

I am an actress – sadly not paid or rewarded for the job. What an Oscar-winning performance i give on a daily basis. Goodness me. I have a strong voice, I have a loud voice, I appear to be 'together' especially when groomed. You always liked me groomed and to this day get incredibly frustrated – not against me but for me – when I don't show my potential to the outside world. Why have I got a low opinion of myself – you are forever telling me how fabulous I am – in intelligence and appearance. I have never been convinced. Having a strong exterior often makes people intimidated – girls possibly envious or think I am more sorted than I am and men – well they don't know what to do.

Leading me on nicely... to your treatment, or that which I have witnessed over the years, of men! You have demanded, nagged, niggled, screamed. I have found this horrendous, aggressive, unnecessary and undoing any potential cosy domestic equilibrium. So much so, that I have become almost a 'recluse' in this said furore of a domestic fight.

Yes, you get the man, he stays, and you create a new 'him' once he is in your life, so much so he is leading a way better lifestyle than he was before!! Actually funny, and you know I think this. However, from my absolute hatred for these outbursts and I know they are from frustration, frustration from their energy, their spinelessness, their inability to understand your demanding princess needs, has led me to internalise every single frustration with a man, for fear of contributing to ugly outbursts. Possibly why I am a 'writer'. You have always encouraged me to write. I am not convinced or driven enough to take it further. Maybe this will change or is on its way to developing to my potential.

Interestingly (putting a positive spin on this!), the inherent fear of not being a nagging fish wife and over-demanding has permitted me to suffer in silence and deny myself my wants and needs, so much so that I am constantly 'in denial' – in denial about a man who is 'worth me', a man with a spine, a day job, material assets, because I thought your demands were too ridiculous, too spoilt brat-like. Quite possibly, I want EXACTLY the same, but have longingly ached for hippies, smellies, ex-addicts, procrastinators, users, weak people.

There is something in me that doesn't – until now – have the prerequisite 'fire in my belly' that I know is vital for appreciating who I am, living my life as I should, knowing who I want and going for it and seeing an opportunity that might enhance myself yet at once, dismiss it. Sometimes I think I am incomplete. Interestingly, this is something I despise in a man. That unwholesome, spineless, weakness of character. Who am I to judge!

I am writing this to you to let you know I adore you, love you, appreciate everything you have done for me and know you have never wanted anything but the genuine best for me. And as someone who believes in fate, know we are 'doing life' as we both should be 'doing life' and i have NO COMPLAINTS. I also know you might possibly have over-compensated our mother-daughter partnership because your mother was such a negative force who didn't allow a friendship between you to occur.

I often think I am so negative in my thoughts about men because I am convinced – interestingly my one focussed conviction – way TOO FOCUSSED – is that they are going to let me down, a la papa?

I now ask you – or fate – to allow me to be me, to be convicted of my convictions and to follow my intuition that only I know, own and am proud of.

Georgina."

Write at least one letter. Surely there is at least one person who has hurt you, yet you believe that the time with them was worthwhile. It might be your dad, your mother, your ex or simply a friend. Write it down until you understand what is it you've learned about yourself from the experience. This letter is only for you, so once you feel you really understand what the relationship gave you, feel free to throw it away. It's in the past now and you've grown. You've grown emotionally and intellectually.

PART FOUR: CHANGE YOUR LIFE FOR THE BETTER

A few words of warning and encouragement

Any changes, good or bad, are going to cause you initial disturbance. We are creatures of habit. When you change, the world around you will take time to adjust. Or if it doesn't, sometimes you need to adjust the world around you i.e. move to new and better surroundings.

You need to change first. In fact, 'change' isn't the right word. Life isn't about changes. Life is ever-evolving. It's a continuous process.

By liberating yourself from the prison of your own emotions as well as breaking free from the social structure you have worked so hard to build around yourself, will start noticing different things and opportunities around you.

Don't force anyone around you to change. It's not about them. It's about you. You came into the life you're living by your own will and you can do whatever you want to do.

As a matter of fact, you not only chose to come here by your own free will. You are one of very few people who is strong and brave enough to experiment and try to make your life bigger and brighter and more beautiful.

You are extremely strong. Many aren't willing to challenge themselves as you are doing here.

Your life didn't come to you with a set of rules. Your life didn't come to you with an understanding of what's right what's wrong (you may know now, but you've learned this over the years based around what others have told you). Life's answers don't always stay the same, it is evolving every day. The thing is, life isn't about answers. It's painful to acknowledge, because often we feel more comfortable if we can know something for certain. But we can't always have that luxury. Not if we want more out of life and to experience something bigger.

Human life has moved beyond just staying alive and reproducing. Those things are becoming easier for most of the world, leaving you more free to do what you want to do.

You may not know at this stage what you want to do, but you are willing to experiment.

While some may have come here with a clear idea of what they wanted to try, no one really has the final answers – because there are none. We are all co-creators. Your actions do affect others and their actions inevitably affect you. We can speculate about the outcome based on our collective knowledge and most importantly, our new-formed beliefs. However - that doesn't make it the truth. This is why the 'Guinness Book of Records' exists. Any belief will be eventually challenged and every record broken.

You are what you are. A very unique and a brave soul, who came into this physical world to enjoy everything it has to offer and to create and experiment further. You are contributing to the development of the universe. While this may sound grand, if you can grasp and accept the idea that everything is moving, you'll accept that your development will help others to develop. No matter how low or high, rich or poor you may feel at the moment. You are important.

You are not alone

No matter how loved or how lonely you may feel at this moment. You are never ever alone, you are never unloved, you are never unprotected - unless you choose to believe so.

Emotions are a very powerful and a truly phenomenal instrument. Once you learn to understand them and, most importantly, not to control them (the minute you try control emotions, you give them more attention hence increasing their power over you) but to CHOOSE them, then you'll see what I am trying to explain here. In many ways, experience cannot be learned or explained, you need to live it for yourself.

For now all you need to know and accept is how unique and strong and special you are. You need to accept yourself. For whatever you believe, whatever's inside you, will be projected outwards.

We are such visual beings that we always look for instant proof, we want visual evidence before we can truly believe. You are the creator. The world and the circumstances around you will adjust. It may take time, but it will adjust.

Your free will is what you've come here with. It's your own. You can't give it away unless you choose so. You are not only strong and unique, you have an ability to create. What you create will depend on the others that you come into contact with, but create you will.

It might be difficult for you to accept right now that you are not alone. Please remember that you are not alone - ever. You are so special. You have more help and strength within you than you realise.

Sometimes you do need to ask for this help. There is nothing wrong with asking. There are many creators who find their emotional satisfaction by helping others. Anyone ever worked for a charity? I did. Who won first of all? You, or in my case it was me. It gives us a sense of empowerment. A sense of being in control. A sense of being strong and being able to help others. Those emotions are priceless.

You do not necessarily need to work for a charity to feel like this. You probably help others already. Maybe you have helped a neighbour by taking in his or her parcel while they were away. Or maybe you brought a cup of coffee to your co-worker to cheer him or her up. You help others every day. You maybe forget to acknowledge that. Take the time to recognize the good that you do.

And the same goes for others. By letting them help you - you empower them. Not everyone will or should help. There are many things that only you can do for yourself. However should you feel in need, there is nothing wrong with asking for help.

You are always loved. You may not realise it, but no matter how bad or unloved you feel at any specific moment, there is always someone who really and truly loves you. They may not be physically next to you right now, but they still love you. However, it's important to remember that you can't choose to be loved by a particular person, for they have the same freedom as you do - freedom of choice.

You are always loved. It's very unfair to say that no one loves you. You hurt those who love you by making a statement like that, and they do not deserve it. You are trying to deny, or hold back the very flow of love coming your way. You are always loved. Whether you see it or not, whether you feel it or not - you are always loved.

You might choose to believe you are not loved, but you are. There is always an abundance of love around you. It's yours should you choose to accept such powerful knowledge that you are always surrounded by love. Love does not differentiate you by your social status. You can be a criminal, you can be that drunken low life scam lying on the street, you can be the CEO of a large corporation, who is truly hated by those who work for you, but you are always loved by someone.

You just need to learn to accept it. You start it by loving yourself. Say to yourself 'I recognise that I am loved'. By doing this you open the tap of love, so it flows freely into your life. Just because you deliberately keep your tap closed, it doesn't mean the water, (apologies, love!) isn't there.

Why should you not love and respect yourself? You are one of very few beings who has decided to come to this 'life' and accept it, with all the pain you may experience. You, by existing here, are already contributing to the development of life itself.

You are so amazing! You are so rare! You are absolutely unbelievable and so fascinating. There is so much to you. Even if you are not using all of your talents to their full potential right now. You are truly magnificent. You are a real magician in this life. Just because time isn't an entity you feel you can control, it does not mean your actions go unnoticed. They do not. Your actions, no matter how big or small, are all very, very important. You may not be Harry Potter, but you still are one of the biggest magicians of the universe. You act and create. Every step of your life is magic.

Now, I never said every bit of magic is good... Yet every action or step you take is definitely a magical one. Which direction you take – that's up to you. One way or another you are already influencing the world. No action of yours will stay unnoticed, no action of yours will fail to influence the rest of the world. That's how powerful you are.

You and I are different people

You know that. I just thought it would be good to remind you. I am sharing a lot of personal details from my life here in order to connect with you.

Please acknowledge and recognise, while we may be similar in some ways, some parts of your life are unique and just yours.

No one else, not me, not your parents, no one else - I repeat – no one else has that something which makes you so special and unique. While you might not feel that way right now, we are similar in some ways and very different and unique in others.

In order to recognise what makes you unique – in terms of your abilities, your qualities - you need to be start being honest. Not with others necessarily. No one will ever really know exactly how you feel, it's your own private experience. While at some stages of life we connect with each other and we truly enjoy that shared experience, most of your feelings and the way you experience various events are yours and only.

Let's be honest

Being honest with others, at this stage... I wouldn't encourage it. I would probably even warn you not to share the changes you're making in your life at all and at the moment. The people around you are not learning this new way of being. You are.

Start being honest with yourself – as it's likely you've not been entirely honest so far. I am not blaming you, I am sometimes not honest with myself simply because I am busy with other stuff and I'd rather close my mind to those issues.

Let me give you an example, so you start understanding what is it exactly that I mean here. Let's say you go to a restaurant and you order gluten-free food. Ask yourself why is it exactly do you order the gluten-free food?

Do you really have a gluten intolerance? According to the latest data there is a very small percentage of people who are really and truly gluten intolerant. Or is it that you read an article that says that gluten is bad for you?

Next time you are in the restaurant, think about it. Do you avoid some foods for one reason but pretend to yourself that it's for a different reason?

Why is it exactly you ask the waiter not to serve you x, y or z?

I mean you may be ok with gluten, but you may prefer not to eat chips because you assume they'll make you fat.

This is where you can really acknowledge your thought processes and start being honest.

If you are not sure, then play with the idea for a while. If you realise that you simply don't like the taste of nuts in your food, just start being honest with yourself and simply tell the waiter you do not like nuts. Do not lie and say you are allergic because you think that's more acceptable.

Happiness

Happiness is not about building a happy family, making babies, raising children. I understand I'll upset many of you by making a statement like that and I want you to know that I think family life is important, but that's not the only way to approach your life. At least not any longer.

We evolve. Life never stays still. Life evolves and we evolve. When we first started creating and acquired our current physical shape, we took time to learn to look after our body. By that I mean we had to learn to stay 'alive' in in the way that we are now familiar.

I'm not referring to philosophy or any eastern teachings here, I'm simply talking about staying physically alive. Not dying. We also have a need to reproduce (make love) in order to sustain our kind.

I honestly believe we are on our way to a unisex world. Yes there are differences in energies between 'men' and 'women'. These are the words we currently use to differentiate them. I believe that soon we will create new words. It's nothing personal, dear Dr Freud, especially considering how I was brought up on your books and used to often refer to your writing when looking for answers. Freud may have been right at the time, but he isn't right anymore.

We have moved on, and now risk using the family unit as a false understanding of 'security'. We are becoming more individual than ever, so for those who want to live in a community or family group, we need to evolve our communication skills and develop a higher respect for our own life desires. I'll be the first to admit that, while I try to practise what I preach, I am totally on your side. I'd just rather have a family and also continue a power struggle, pursuing my own desires ☺

I mean, who doesn't want to have nice holidays where everything is taken care of, just for you and at no expense to you. You don't even have to lift a finger, you just wink and a well-toned young creature called 'waitress' delivers your favourite cocktail....

Wait did I say 'wink'...? No that's too complicated. Maybe they can simply read your mind! Ah - that's what I am talking about. We do want everything to be about us, whether we acknowledge that publically or not.

Of course if you really believe that your needs are different, you can join the rest of us hypocrites and say, 'I don't want a free holiday, my family have always worked hard and I never want anything for nothing...'

But what happens when your husband or wife leaves you?

There you are with a child on your hands, unable to make ends meet, and with your child constantly asking you 'Mummy! Where's Daddy?'

Maybe you start dating another guy who brings your child presents. And gifts to you, or maybe covers your bills occasionally. And yes, you hope he might propose you. Do you really love the guy that much? Are you really, honestly doing it for your child?

There we go. While you might not have experienced this exact scenario, you still recognize it. That's the moment when your comfort zone 'switch' turns on and you are no longer willing to face the truth.

Welcome! You've just joined the army of hypocrites that I call the human race. Lovely.

Why would you want to face your true feelings or recognize your true desires, when it is soooo much easier to follow the path everyone has gone through, where you know exactly what to expect?

How can you possibly know that tomorrow you will be given a new job promotion with a higher salary and that your very partner will no longer seem as worthwhile. Or, how can you be sure that tomorrow you won't end up flying to Mars, meet another human – correction, Martian - who looks so much better than your current partner?

Ok, let's slow down.

How do you know for sure that you'll go to your local coffee shop, where you regularly get your drink... and that they'll serve you exactly the same drink with exactly the same taste, day after day?

You don't. The fact is, you never ever know anything for sure. You know why? You haven't explored enough to realise that nothing is ever certain. You have become a dependent co-creator. You no longer belong to yourself.

You are a SLAVE. Surprised? Why? Why did you go to school? Because you were told to go by your parents.

Why did you get the job you did? Most probably because you were told that's what people do. That's what a life is.

Why do you want to have a girlfriend or a boyfriend? Ah, this is unfair - that's biological, right? Then why do you want to get married? If you're not the 'marrying type' then why are you staying with your partner? Did he or she tell you they aren't really the marrying kind either? Keep your switch set to the 'comfort zone'... Be my guest.

And please don't defend yourself by saying that you love each other. You may, there are truly happy couples out there. I've met them, and I have my own life as evidence. However for the majority, it is a convenience that you cover up with the word 'love'. It doesn't matter if you lie to me, as long as you are honest with yourself.

And I bet you aren't being entirely honest. You probably call it human nature. I call it keeping your comfort zone switched on.

In my family, there's a saying that 'you can never call a good place a ZONE'. I'm not sure about other languages but in a country which no longer exists, the USSR, that word was used to describe places where people were kept against their own will (that's probably quite an accurate description of your comfort zone – because, do you want to be there, really?).

Aren't you working hard to create your false security, your 'comfort' zone. Or is it more of a discomfort zone, if you're honest with yourself?

I feel like I should take a break here and be nice to you for a while.

But wait, why should I? Why should I be nice to someone who is unappreciative of themselves? After all it's your life... What do I care? Why should I be nice to you when you deliberately do everything you can to enslave yourself and cancel yourself out – denying the real amazing person that you are?

Why should I, when you work so hard to mimic others' success, rather than create your own?

Why should I, when you marry someone you don't love, for convenience, or just because that's what you think it is RIGHT or that's what your parents want from you?

Why should I, when you work for a company, which literally pays your bills... yet you curse every day that you have to go into work? Ask yourself, why did you apply for the job in the first place if you didn't want it?

But let's stay on course. Happiness. Maybe in the past, you felt like you needed a partner in order to survive. However if you are reading this book, you are ready to wake up. Life is not a sleepy dream.

Life is very much real, it is a manifestation of real energy, made up of your thoughts, your ideas your emotions. You are very real. You can be by yourself. And you can create by yourself (as much as it is possible at all). Though I agree that to create together is much more fun!

Now, whether you are a single-minded creator or you prefer to co-create, you still need to wake up and learn what it is that you really are.

This is particularly true if you are the helpful kind. If you believe that your true purpose is ONLY helping others - for example, working for a charity because it helps so many people and makes them happy. Yes, it probably does, but primarily, it helps you to feel better. You get your energy boost and set your satisfaction levels high, because of helping others. You still need to learn what it is YOU bring to the table or, speaking the Life Language, to the co-creative process.

The emotion that produces LOVE and happiness is a 'green light' to your creative process, as long as it's produced on its own and does not depend on others involvement. However, if two people produce the same emotion for the same purpose independent of each other – this is when creative power can really flow, and the real progress occurs.

The finale

'What joy would life provide us with, if not for the beauty of its complications?'

The most interesting part of the work that I do is that I acknowledge and respect past events; yet I treat them as though they are absolutely irrelevant to our future possibilities. The past is a great source of strength and power as well as the love we all crave. And yes, some of them – those loves in the past - were absolutely amazing and memorable, yet life continues without them and is constantly moving.

The important part is to acknowledge that all the actions you take should be thought through, since any creation produces side effects, and sometimes unintended consequences.

We each influence each other and the rest of the world whether we are aware of it or not. Our actions are like a form of medicine. We might produce something that treats a particular disease, but the medicine also produces side effects we did not ask for, or have not have anticipated.

Anything you create will have unintended consequences and side effects. That is the pure chemistry of a basic chain reaction, but on a global scale.

I understand that it's painful to be aware of the impact your life has on so many of us. Often it is easier to simply refer to something you've learned from psychology lessons rather than create your own experiences and choose your own emotions. But psychology is merely a database for what has happened so far, it is not a prediction for the future.

It's real Art. It's Life.

As Marilyn Monroe used to sing in 'There's No Business Like Showbusiness': 'After you get what you want you don't want it... Changeable, you've got a changeable nature...'

Keep wanting, keep leaving, keep enjoying and keep taking whatever it is you want from this life. That might be using your creative power to create something else, it might be breathing in the scent of flowers or simply taking the sounds of the music into your ears… Enjoy living.

Olga xxx

PART FIVE: SUCCESS IS CONTAGIOUS TOO

Here are a few stories from people who've either worked with me or explored the ideas outlined in this book.

Please read on, the success of others is contagious, enjoyable and can help support and inspire you to make changes to your own life.

What my lovely client **G.R.** said about working with me:

"... Through your mantras, from spending hours of coaching with you I have learnt to flip any negative thoughts 180 degrees to transform them into a positive.

Rather than declaring, 'why not me, why haven't I met my life partner, why am I so stressed about not being with a boyfriend etc etc' with continuous self-harming inner dialogue, I have finally seen the light.

More than that, apart from just being aware of how toxic are these emotion-heavy-thought-processes, do any of us really acknowledge how detrimental they are to happiness?

We know they are not great thought patterns, if we weren't born yesterday and if we can think. We know full well they are ridiculous and make us moody people to be around. I have gone that further stage and acknowledged AND REMEMBERED to flip them.

It is so easy to 'see how it works', and think hey, I've 'got this self-help mantra stuff' down to a tee and wake each morning and go to sleep each night reminding ourselves how fabulous we are. But do we actually action the process of turning them around and lightening the load? Do we, really? It is so easy to say, hey I'm great and I'm loved and I'm going to be fine and I am good at this and that and the other'.

Yet the more we repeat this, the more we drill this into our mind, make it a new way of making our brain work, it ultimately gets hammered in tightly and it evolves into a natural tendency to make this negative into a positive. Not every time, not every day, I'm no robot (sadly this is true!) yet the monotony finally 'clicked' into the wiring of my brain and I think, from my gut if I am honest, that we humans do definitely control our emotions. A sensitive thing since my memory began, I've always been delicate, on the inside, hard as nails on the outside – weeping uncontrollably when 'friends' let me down (now I am older, maybe it was envy on their part, maybe bullying or maybe just normal little girl yukky natural behavior). Whatever it was, decades of my life have been gobbled up, never to be seen again, with far too much self-absorbed angst making my bones ache, my tummy feeble and my sleep inconsistent.

Finally I can tell my mind to SHUT THE F**K UP and it is incredible. It is a breakthrough. It is fulfilling and you know what, no regrets because it has made me strong, made me see the funny side even though there were some truly truly horrific moments and me realize how strong my inner core is, which I always knew. I am so sensitive to other people's negative energy, it allowed my life not to evolve as smoothly as it should. It hindered, it put a sad cup-half-empty slant on my day-to-day existence.

Now, I am not saying this: I am now a utopian human whose life will now be a pretty meadow with perfect sunshine that doesn't make my skin wrinkly. But it sure as hell will lighten the daily load in this crazy existential life we lead.

After all, those of us who think too much, do need a kick up the butt at times and we need to wake up, smell the coffee and realize that 'verbal diarrhoea' – the phrase coined so beautifully by Ms Levancuka and shouted loudly in my direction countless times– sets us backwards into the past, creating misery and preventing one from enjoying being alive and moving forwards.

A few words from my fabulous client **J.D**

"Hi Olga,

It's some time after we've had our sessions together. Back then I had my doubts. Now…

Now, I'm sat in the kitchen at a solid wood table that sits 8 to 10 people. The dishwasher is on and cleaning the dishes from the dinner I shared with my family and friends the night before. I now live in a house with 5 bedrooms outside of London which I share with my husband, two children and our Labrador dog. (Remember my 1 bedroom house I could not afford to live in?)

The house is now large enough that I can invite the whole family over for Christmas and holidays and although well presented it is a relaxed eclectic environment.

It's a clear crisp day where the air smells slightly damp and cold but is invigorating. I am sat working on my website which is firmly established with funding and I'm currently working on a book deal.

My husband and I are very close and enjoy having time together with the children and on our own. He also has a large circle of friends as do I. We often all get together in large groups for evenings or outings.

My husband makes me laugh and he's attentive to the small things that make me smile. He's a good conversationalist and we never run out of things to talk about other than when we're comfortable in our own restful silence together. We are strongly attracted to each other and deeply in love.

I feel lucky and happy. I smile knowing that I have finally found a partner who appreciates me and I feel truly confident and able to fulfil my potential as a wife, a mother and business women in my own right.

We are financially stable and can afford to go on holidays to far flung places and to provide security for our children and their education.

I am able to offer financial support to friends and family who have been supportive to me over the years and I am working with a woman's charity at least one day a week to help raise awareness and funds. My husband and I are discussing the possibility of adopting a child.

At last, I feel relaxed, proud, secure, loved and I am happy.

A week ago one of my best friends from university called me to say she had a business idea and she wants me to do it with her. She is a mum and not working and wants a project. Her website idea had a few holes in it and I shared mine which she loved. She wants to help me get it up and running and has experience of business planning etc. We've said we'll get together in a couple of weeks to write the business plan together. At first I was a little resistant thinking the idea was "mine" and not want to lose control but I've also thought that I've had time to do it my own and not done enough to progress it. This way I've got someone pushing forward and pushing me forward too. Your thoughts would be appreciated, Olga!"

And one more, from my inspiring client **M.P.**

"It's amazing how sometimes you can re-emerge as a different person due to certain events in your life... Have you experienced that?

After being controlled for many years, I was not allowed to be ME. Just over two years ago it changed, I went it alone, on my own, and yes, as hard it was, I done it. I became ME, the real ME.

This became easier as time went on, especially after meeting Olga, by chance or by luck? Since meeting with Olga, things have changed, my life is more calm, things happen by nature, organically.

Just a social chat, at times with Olga makes such a difference, I leave such an inspired person.

After meeting with Olga on two or three ocassions, socially, it became quite evident that this was the person who could really bring out the best in me, so, I eventually went on one of her workshops, and wow, what an experience, the 'being at peace' with myself became even stronger. This made an even bigger change to the way I am. I now allow things to happen, I don't chase the outcome that I want, and by doing so it has had a greater effect on my business and relationships with others.

I am now very much my own person, the person who I am, and like. Business has also improved, I now have a regular turnover of work and cover my costs/living expenses.

To me, having engaged with Olga has proved to be invaluable, many people have professed to be of help, but no one, with exception of Olga, has actually delivered and made me understand, who I am, and where I am going."

"Well... I was thinking how to start my story and to be honest with you – I still don't know. But what I know for sure is that I really wanted to show by example how we can change things in our lives for better or at least make it different. Make it the way we WANT it to be.

I've known Olga for a long time now and from time to time we are having a great time and talk which – I hope – we both enjoy very much. For me our meetings are always inspiring. It is a privilege to be asked to write just a few words for her new book. Thank you Olga!

This story could easily be assigned to almost each chapter – on money, on emotions, on religion, on body...

I lived in London for years and as probably everyone has, I had a great times and not so great times. Ups and downs. Life, eehh?! I couldn't complain much – always had a good job in fashion industry. First years I was sharing flats with some other people to save some money and later on I decided to live on my own. It was a luxury!

Having a one bedroom flat just for myself!!! I was paying a lot for it – of course not as much as for a flat in Knightsbridge but still! And I have decided to open my business in partnership with my friend – a very good friend. She is a very good person but unfortunately at that time we started our company she lost her way – she started to drink a lot and she got herself into some kind of trouble and she took a huge loan for our company – forgetting to tell me.

Anyway – making this story short – by this time I didn't have any money, just debts! I started to work again for fashion designers just to make some cash for bills. I had one thought in my mind– I never ever again will be living in a shared flat.

The only place I can move to from my one bedroom flat is my OWN place. I believed it but real life wasn't so optimistic. I could hardly pay my bills and rent not to mention paying off the loan. I didn't even think of going shopping just for pleasure, to spend some money on shoes or clothes. I was soooo depressed.

I always wanted to have a comfortable life, to have money for almost everything – and I didn't have even seven pounds for the cinema! I always knew money does not give happiness but maybe it can buy happiness!!! :)

Anyway I was trying to figure it out how to live... at that time no one knew about my troubles – I am the kind of person who does not share her life with everyone – even the closest friends.

So as always I asked Olga for a meeting because as I have mentioned before we saw each other from time to time socially. And as always we had a great time – I remember well – we had breakfast in a nice Italian restaurant near Sloane Square. She had porridge which looked absolutely horrible and she loved it!:) Maybe that is why I remember it so well!

We talked a lot about her studies and the ideology she is into and I gave her my journal to write me some of her exercises. Guess what, a few days ago I found this journal!!! She asked me to keep repeating every day what she wrote:

'I am what I am!

I am getting younger every day!

I am getting healthier every day!

I am getting richer every day!

My financial situation is constantly improving!

Love

Success

Power

Luck

Happiness

'Dear God thank you thank you thank you for everything!'

'My dear angels thank you thank you thank you for all the support and help you are giving me everyday!'

She also asked me to make a collage of things I want to have in my life and keep it near me, but not show it to anyone.

So I came back to my flat and I did it. I kept it next to my bed in a drawer and every night I was looking at it and repeating every word!

I think I forgot to mention to you that I didn't tell Olga about my problems – til now! :)

After this meeting I was so positive, my confidence grew so much! In two years after that breakfast so many good things happened to me, so many things changed for the better!

If you are thinking I am out of debt and have a nice job I will tell you – it's even better!:) I bought my OWN flat which I love, I have a new company and I love it, I still have my collage next to my bed and I love it! :) I love it because I still have a few things to achieve and I know I will get them sooner or later. My life will be great! Ooohhh nooooo – my life IS great!!!

I do believe that we can change everything in our lives. Everything can be the way we want it! I always knew it somehow, but I wasn't sure about it til I had the best breakfast of my life at this Italian restaurant!"

PART SIX: EMOTIONAL EXERCISES TO TRY

Fun exercise ☺

I call this the pre-exercise, and I think you'll love it!

Please take a note from your own wallet if you are a retro-conformist who carries cash ;). For those fully modernized human beings among you, go to the nearest cash machine and withdraw a paper-note of small but substantial value. For example $100 dollar bill or £50 pounds – even a £10 note will do. Wherever you are, work out the amount of money that you are happy to play with.

Got the note?

Now remember:

'Life is a game that must be played'

Edwin Arlington Robinson

Let's play!

Fold your note once.

Have a look at it and ask yourself – is it still the same note that the shops would accept as payment?

Obviously, yes.

Fold your note as many times as you can.

Now look at it again. Would the shop still accept it now, in exchange for something you'd like to purchase?

Obviously, yes. The sales assistant may give you a funny look, but they will still accept it.

Now stamp on the note, and walk on it for a bit. Then pick it up and ask yourself, would the note still be accepted?

And please don't be a smart ass here… I am well aware of the fact that if you are playing with a foreign note, in a country where it isn't the accepted currency then a shop won't accept it or they'll exchange it for a lesser value. We are playing here with the currency in use in your own country.

What do you say? Will they accept the 'stepped all-over' note now as a part of the payment?

Of course they will! It's money!

I think I should probably get my point across, before you ruin your note and I make you cry while you are trying to stick it back together with sellotape... !

But guess what – even if it's sellotaped together, the note will still be worth the same. It may only be accepted at the bank, as opposed to in a shop, but nevertheless the value is the same! No matter what you do to it, unless if you burn it (that is – kill it) the value stays unchanged.

I once knew a girl who used to work as a cleaner and she told me how once, she literally washed her boss's money. By mistake of course! She then had to dry and iron it, so that her boss would find the notes washed, clean, dry, ironed and lined up nicely on a table (with a note: 'Sorry, I washed your money').

You see, you are like MONEY!

You really are the same. No matter what you do to money, (unless you 'kill' it by burning it or something similar) the value stays, undiminished. It's the same with you – no matter what happens to you (unless you die and for some, after that their value may even increase) – your value will always stay with you. It will always stay the same.

But it is entirely up to you. It is you who chooses what side to show, the dirty side.... or the valuable side. And what if there are other people with the same 'value' as you? Well guess what, it works the same as with money! The preference always goes to the shinier tenner.

Stick to your value. It will never be diminished unless you choose to diminish it, unless you feel like going to the shop and saying 'I know I have a tenner, but I feel a bit low at the moment, so can I please give you a tenner for this £5 item?' You'd be mad to do that, wouldn't you? Then why do you think of yourself as less valuable that you really are?!

Wash yourself, iron yourself and off you go, showing off your bright and shiny side and knowing your exact value. That is – the valuable and unique human being that you ARE. Enjoy.

Exercise 1

Do not underestimate the power of simplicity. It all starts, from now on, with you. SIMPLE.

Some of you may have guessed correctly that I am talking about affirmations. In case you are not familiar with such terminology, affirmations are a positive statement made in the present time, eg taking into account what we are or what we want to achieve or to become. Putting it differently: Affirmations are your GOALS.

If you would like to have a better understanding of affirmations and a bit of scientific explanation, please refer to Exercise 3 and the explanations following it in my book 'Increase Your Confidence in One Day'. It is a really really great book covering all the basics of self-understanding and self-respect.

And back to affirmations.

Pick few statements focussing on what you want to achieve in life. For example:

'I'd like to be the owner of a large corporation'

or 'I'd like to live in paradise'.

Now study your goals carefully and decide what qualities you would need to achieve that goal.

For example for 'I'd like to be the owner of a large corporation' – it's likely that to achieve that goal you would need confidence, and be decisive, trustworthy or not (you choose!), smart and lucky.

For 'I'd like to live in paradise' – to live in paradise you would probably need to be relaxed, adventurous, carefree and pretty self-sufficient, as you'd need to know how to look after yourself on a deserted island.

Please note the above statements are only examples, it may well be that your goals, and the qualities you associate with them may be different.

Now that you have your goals and the qualities that go with them, let's have a look at the qualities you possess already. For example, if you are already trustworthy – that could be one of your affirmations:

'I am trustworthy.'

If you are already adventurous, that could be one of your affirmations:

'I am adventurous.'

Go through each quality that goes with your goal, think about whether you possess it already and form the affirmation accordingly.

Now we have:

'I am trustworthy.'

'I am adventurous.'

Now let's go through the qualities you need for your goals, that you don't believe you have yet. What do you need to achieve in order to reach your goal? For example, if you would like to be the owner of a large corporation, then you probably need to work as a manager first. Which qualities are required of a manager? Write them down. Please note, we are looking at the qualities YOU BELIEVE a manager needs to have – not just what others tell you.

Now go carefully through each quality and identify which ones you possess already. Here you'll need to be somewhat creative. For example, if you believe that time-keeping is an important quality, and you know that you are always late for work but you ARE always on time for meeting your older brother, then you do possess this quality. You just choose to use it at times that suit you and your life. But what is important is that you CHOOSE this – and you do have this quality in you already. Which means that it is a true statement and therefore an affirmation. You can now add this to our affirmation list:

'I am always on time.'

Yes, the fact that you are not always on time is your choice. Should you choose to be on time – this affirmation will not only be relevant to your goal, but also completely true.

I would like to go a bit further here, and play with a big statement like 'I am loved'. For example, you might be looking for a partner but haven't been dating for at least three years (I've had clients like this, and let me tell you, they were very handsome and very eligible). Your final goal would be: 'I am in relationship'. The quality you'd possess would be 'I am loved'.

You are definitely not feeling it at the moment because you haven't found that perfect person yet. So you assume that you are not loved. Now I'd like you to pick one person who loves you unconditionally. Even if that is only your grandmother – that is irrelevant. If you feel particularly sarcastic or lonely then you can even pick your dog or goldfish. Voilà – you can now say that 'I am loved'.

You need feelings, you need to feel that emotion. Who gives you the chance to feel loved at this given moment is absolutely irrelevant. You have to start experiencing before you have it.

Here you go - you've got four affirmations so far:

'I am trustworthy.'

'I am adventurous.'

'I am always on time.'

AND

'I am loved.'

Keep repeating your affirmations every time you are bored, on your way to school, work or meeting new people and once you get used to them and you find it fun – start experimenting and creating new affirmations.

I also run one-to-one affirmation formation sessions, so if you need further help or you are working on a very precise goals, please contact me via www.SkinnyRichCoach.com to book your session. Don't underestimate the power of simple things. It's like that butterfly who flaps its wings in one place, and that alone produces a hurricane across the continent. Be that butterfly. Start flapping your wings.

Exercise 2

This particular exercise is for those of you who have issues regarding money, whether that's because you never have enough, or because you have too much and experience feelings of guilt. While most people believe you can never have too much money, I've worked with many people whose problems could be traced back to inheriting a large sum of money and feeling guilty about his or her inheritance. If you belong to this group of people, it's possible that you are blighted by feelings of doubt, and fear that much of your success and popularity are the result of someone else's good fortune and not of your own doing. The other side to this situation is that people who don't need to work can have difficulties finding something worthwhile to do with their time, and can end up feeling useless.

The exercise is indirect, but has a rather complex structure. Just go along with it, even if you feel uncomfortable or if you are having a hard time at the moment - see what happens just after a month ☺

Let's start.

Think back to your early childhood, when you started to think about what you wanted to become when you grew up. Ignore what you have achieved or not at this particular stage, just remember one of those moments when you were considering your future as an adult. Many may remember they dreamt that they would be the world's best horse-rider, or maybe a pianist. Some of my classmates dreamt of becoming a nurse because they wanted to help ill people, while some of the boys wanted to become a pilot because that would show what a big man they are. What was it you dreamed about? It doesn't even matter at this stage whether it was a pirate or a drug-dealer that you wanted to become! Really!

Now think - remember how you felt when you were saying 'I am going to be............' Probably the feelings were of excitement, adventure or importance. You probably felt really happy about the possibilities awaiting you? I can't possibly predict your thoughts as you are performing the exercise, but I think it's likely that whatever it is you wanted to be, even if it was a rich financier, the emotions you experienced were not regarding the amount of money you might have. You were experiencing emotions of excitement and adventure and you probably felt really happy dreaming of all the opportunities awaiting you.

Jot down your feelings and emotions, for example:

Excitement

Feeling happy

Feeling important

Now, wherever you are now, at this very moment, find what would provoke those same emotions in you. Is it looking at your puppy wagging its tail and wanting to play? Is it knowing that you are safe and comfortable in your well looked-after home? Are you happy because you've looked at a photo of you with your friends during that skiing trip, the one where you met the One? Or is it that you have realized you will have a spare hour or so tonight to read your favourite novel?

Even if it is something like feeling really excited that the building works next door have stopped. Find something right now that makes you experience the very same emotions you did when you were small and dreaming of your exciting future. Or watch your favourite comedy, have a good laugh and then perform this exercise again. You might notice something else. It may be that knowing that you are providing for your child makes you feel important and that your efforts are worthwhile.

Please repeat this exercise at least twice a day till you learn to divert your attention to objects or events which feed your desired emotions. Then simply learn to experience these beautiful emotions as often as you can or at least every couple of hours during the day. You may even start writing a diary of events or objects which feed your excitement or make you feel happy. If you are a visual person – take photos of such events or objects and write on the back a note about the amazing and happy feelings you experience when you look at them.

Exercise 3

This exercise is for when you do not have enough money.

The time frame you allocate for this exercise should also include time for Exercise 2, as they work together.

Most people have had one of those grey days, when you receive your post and open it to find an overdue payment or a completely unexpected bill for tax. It becomes worse if you were saving for a holiday and now you can say goodbye to that idea as you have to use funds to cover your bills.

Or it could be that you receive a paycheck and you notice that the amount is smaller than you were expecting, or worse yet, it is the amount you were expecting but you know it is nowhere near enough to cover the bills you need to pay during the next week or two.

As paradoxical it sounds, no matter how much money you may earn now, you'll never feel completely satisfied with what you have. Even with huge amounts of money, you might be happy at first, but soon you'll go backwards and feel angry or frustrated that the amount is not enough after all.

Money is like your body. Whether there is enough or not you still need to respect and look after it. In a sense, you do not want to run out of 'petrol' for your car (referring to your actual body here) do you?

Here is the exercise. Every time you receive a sum of money, no matter how small or big, you now need to feel happy about money coming into your life. From now on, any time you receive a payslip, in your mind, thank the money for coming your way (after all the company you work for could run into troubles and be unable to pay you on time). Spend time enjoying feeling the money in your hands and seeing it in your account.

Show your honest appreciation towards the flow of money in your life. Should you find money on the street or a parent gives you a little extra for your birthday or you receive a bonus at work – run home and start dancing (make sure you are alone so no one thinks your sanity is at risk – or give them this book) with excitement. Celebrate the fact that you weren't expecting this money, yet somehow it found its way into your life. So now you know - whether you expect it or not, because you respect and love money (but aren't attached to money - big difference!) somehow money finds its way into your life. Do this for at least three to six months, in conjunction with Exercise 2.

Next step. Money is not responsible for your mismanagement of funds, or any misfortunes you have suffered. Money really works hard on your behalf. Any new bill that comes your way, think of a way either to pay straight up, or temporarily cut down your expenses or save up in order to pay the debt. All this has to be dealt with using a very practical attitude and with no emotions attached. Should you need to – seek help. The government runs free advisory centres to help you handle debts.

Meanwhile, don't let yourself fall back into the emotional state of 'no matter how hard I work, the money is never enough.' From now on you are forbidden to feel that emotion, but if you can't get it out of your head, keep repeating in your mind:

'I don't know quite know the way yet, but I am definitely coming up with the right solutions. I am not only managing my money wisely, I am learning to accumulate money too.'

Stick with this attitude, and soon you will be saying 'How did I manage to save £2000, last year?! Wow, now I have some extra money – in case I feel like indulging myself.'

Take £50 from that fund to spend as you wish! (Even if it's as simple as buying every single kid of yours three ice creams each). Make it your goal to save another £2000 during the next six months and then take a holiday, or do whatever else you wanted to save some money for.

But remember, this exercise only works if you do it simultaneously with Exercise 2. And stick with it!

Exercise 4

Learn to appreciate people around you rather than driving them away. You can never succeed alone. Unless that is what you want – to live alone, succeed alone and not have anyone around you.

From now on, every time you want to start a conversation, or fill an awkward silence, start with something along these lines:

'What a lovely weather today!'

'I love your coat'

'Did you read that exciting article about... (make sure you have another sentence ready to save the stranger from an uncomfortable situation if they haven't read it).'

Or feel free to practice and come up with your own phrases that make other people at ease with you. Even if it is as simple as just smiling at someone rather than starting a conversation.

The point here is that from now on you should never ever use phrases like:

- 'What's wrong?'
- 'What's with your face?'
- 'What's happening?'
- 'Why did you do that?'
- 'What's wrong with you?'
- 'Why are you like this?'

Not only are they offensive, they put other people on 'guard'. Hence it's more difficult to communicate with them at a later stage, or worse still, they might avoid you altogether. Any conversation generally starting with

'What?' and 'Why?' can seem defensive. You'll save yourself and others from a lot of socially confusing moments by simply starting a conversation, and if the person wants to share something – they will. By themselves. They are much more likely to share if you do not start the conversation with 'What?' and 'Why?'

A note from the Author...

It would be great to hear your feedback as well as how did you benefit from reading this book or how did the information in the book has helped you.

Your input as well as your comments are highly appreciated and valued.

Please send your feedback and stories via www.OlgaLevancuka.com

For author events, please see the blog on www.OlgaLevancuka.com as well as for new book updates.

I am also still taking on private clients for my "Skinny Rich Self" program. Details for that and for my workshops and seminars can be found via www.SkinnyRichCoach.com

If you'd like me to run a communication and relationship session for your company, please contact me via the 'Booking Information' page on www.SkinnyRichCoach.com website.

Otherwise feel free to follow me, quite literally, via twitter where I lavishly post daily insights and thoughts, posing under my coaching name: **@SkinnyRichCoach** ☺

Acknowledgements

In addition to the many people who made this book possible, my special thanks go to Louie Stowell who's given me lots of helpful advice about writing, and challenged my ideas. This woman has long fascinated me with the depth of her knowledge, as well as her seemingly simple yet rare female charm with a hint of mystery. Long before this book came into being, I'd already grown very fond of her. Louie, the rich quality of you as a human being is beyond magnetic.

And thank you for something you said which has imprinted in my mind during that breakfast at Camden Passage in Islington, where you kept me outdoors and feeling rather cold in my flimsy jacket: "…can you be nicer to people?!"

My special thanks go to Alexander Clark. Alex is the humblest genius I've ever met who has helped me to evolve many views regarding language. I would like to draw your attention to his 'Polynomial Identification in the Limit of Substitutable Context-free Languages' article which is simply a breakthrough in the way we perceive the learnability of languages; as well as proof of the long respected yet completely false idea of Chomsky regarding UG (universal grammar). Alex, you will always occupy a very special place in my heart. Thank you for your support and simply being there for me.

Thank you Lottie (Charlotte O'Conor) for believing in me and working so hard on my press exposure. And your ability to lift my spirit at time I thought I was hitting against the wall.

Thank you Sam Merry (luluandlush.com), for sponsoring my workshops and supporting my work in any way you can. Your strengths are inspirational, so much so, that at times I simply want to give you a hug and tuck you up in bed to ensure you get some sleep and rest! I've never seen anyone work as hard as you do and think as much as you do of everyone around you.

Thank you Jason Pavlou from giraffepress.co.uk, Cheryl Laidlaw and Lewis Malka from Diabloms.co.uk, Magda bluedahlia.eu, Juliet Rowe from julietrowe.com and Louise Gardner. It is your support and your acceptance experimenting with some of my suggestions and ideas that helped me to write this book. It is your success that kept me inspired. I wish everyone could be as lucky as I am to be surrounded with such genuine people, who are not just great business people. You are extremely talented yet humble, and I absolutely adore you!

Thank you Gloria Pyne. I will never forget that day I was in Paris in a five star hotel, hiding in a toilet from my partner during our romantic getaway, because I didn't dare to share the events of my life with him. I remember trying to contact you. Your help in dealing with my 'world' is immense and I am forever grateful to you for that help and knowledge you have shared with me.

Gloria is a medium. While I am not the person who believes entirely about the existence of certain energies, the situations that I regularly used to get myself into required attention from someone who could explain the 'weird' events in my life.

And of course my dear parents including my Greek mum, who knew nothing of the project, I was working on. Thank you for your support, help and feeding me from time to time ☺

Also by this author:

Increase Your Confidence in One Day

About the book:

'Increase your Confidence in One Day' explores the true meaning of confidence, and helps readers to unlock their potential, release the fears that are holding them back and make real life changes that will have a strong and lasting effect.

In today's competitive marketplace, confidence is the single most important quality you can have. Confidence can unlock hidden potential and help you be the best you can be in all areas of your life.

'Increase your Confidence in One Day' has already been a life-changing read for thousands of people across the world. Here is what one reader has to say:

"Olga has an amazing talent for change. Whether the change you are looking for is a transformation in the way you manage a company, or a more personal relationship-oriented goal, Olga can deliver. This book is quite inspiring — it's an overused cliché to say that it will change your life, but it just might"

Alex Clark, Lecturer, Royal Holloway, University of London

To discover the secrets of confidence for yourself, go to:
http://amzn.to/swS4u8

Or visit www.OlgaLevancuka.com

30952639R00065

Made in the USA
Middletown, DE
15 April 2016